The Adept Teacher

The Adept Teacher

By

Ruslan Protsiv, Kathryn Protsiv

Teacher Development and Training, UK

Published by The Teacher Development and Training.
Made in The United Kingdom.
2018

Copyright © 2018 by
TEACHER DEVELOPMENT AND TRAINING, LTD

All rights reserved. This book or any portion thereof may not be reproduced or used in any manner whatsoever without the express written permission of the copyright holder, except for the use of brief quotations in a review.

This book is sold subject to the conditions that it shall not, by way of trade or otherwise, be lent, re-sold, hired out or otherwise circulated without the author's prior consent in any form of binding or cover other than that in which it is published and without a similar condition including this condition being imposed on the subsequent purchaser.

The names, characters and events portrayed in this book are fictitious. Any similarity to real persons, living or dead, events or localities is coincidental and not intended by the author.

Cover credit: Created by Jannoon028 - Freepik.com
ISBN-13: 9781729107683

First published in 2018

Contents

Introduction — 9
    A Matter Of Skill — 11
    Making This Book Work For You — 11
Teaching Classroom Routines — 13
    Model What You Expect — 14
    Practise With Pupils — 20
    Reinforce Success — 22
    Modify — 24
    Use Visual And Audio Signals — 25
Routines At The Start Of The Day — 29
    Entering The Classroom — 30
        Lining Up
        Walking Through The School
        Putting Away Belongings
        Settling Down
    Registration — 36
        Activities During The Registration
        Fire Registers
        Dinner Registers
        Morning Prayer
    Daily Schedule — 40
        Displaying The Schedule
        Sharing The Schedule For The Day
    Class Jobs — 42
        Assigning Class Jobs
        Advertising Class Jobs
        Types Of Class Jobs
    Early Morning Work — 47
        Consolidating New Learning
        Responding To Marking
        Peer Support Work
    Handing In Homework — 53
    Communicating With Parents — 54
Lessons — 58
    Carpet Time — 59
        Allocating Carpet Spaces
        Settling Down On The Carpet
        Dismissing Children From The Carpet

Individual Whiteboards	66
Types Of Activities With Whiteboards	
Distributing Whiteboards	
Handling Resources	73
Externally Held Resources	
Resources Held In The Classroom	
Asking And Answering Questions	77
Teacher Asking Questions	
Children Answering Questions	
Pupils Asking Questions	
Transitions Between Activities	86
Whole Class Transition	
Group Transition	
Individual Transition	
Peer And Self-Assessment	100
Self-Assessment Vs Self-Marking	
Self-Assessment	
Peer Assessment	
Tidying Up	111
Breaks	113
Small Breaks	114
Rest Time In Early Years	115
Toilet Breaks	117
Lining Up	119
Snack Time	124
End Of The Day	129
Summing Up The Day	129
Summing Up What Has Been Learned	
Say What Needs To Improve	
Sending Them Happy	
Getting Ready To Leave	133
Homework	
Letters	
Accident Slips	
Collecting Belongings	
Putting On Coats	
Orderly Dismissal	140
Dismissing To The Right Person	
Children Who Are Not Collected On Time	
After School Clubs	
A Final Word	145

To

All teachers – past, present and future.

With special thanks to Mrs Quaye – the teacher who inspired love of learning as both a tool to achieve goals and the most enjoyable pastime.

A WORD FROM THE AUTHORS

Educational excellence can only be achieved by exceptionally effective teachers who, together with many other skills, are trained to be highly organised and efficient.

After a combined total of over 30 years of experience in diverse and challenging schools of inner London city, first as class teachers, then middle and senior leaders of schools, we have come to a conclusion – teachers are great when they continuously train to improve their practice. They are great when they understand what they are doing and even greater when they know why.

This book is a toolkit for any teacher looking to create an efficient, effective and organised classroom that allows them to focus on the many pressing demands teaching in the modern school will give. The chapters are designed to be easy to follow, clear and concise - a practical guide for the time-pressured teachers.

Ruslan Protsiv is an experienced headteacher of a primary school in London, UK.

Kathryn Protsiv is a former teacher, special needs coordinator and a deputy headteacher of a primary school in London, UK.

INTRODUCTION

Productivity is never an accident. It is always the result of a commitment to excellence, intelligent planning, and focused effort.

PAUL J. MEYER

If you are fortunate enough, you would have received a first-class teacher training. Thus, it is easy to imagine your tutors having extensive experience and deep knowledge of classroom practice which they skilfully shared with you. Having learned from the wealth of their experiences, you stepped into the classroom yourself as a student teacher. Mentors at your placement schools were outstanding teachers. They always had time for you, showed and explained all you needed to know and gently guided you to become as good as they were. After a short time, you applied for your first teaching job. It was not long before you were invited to an interview. With the knowledge and skills acquired throughout your training, you easily secured your first job as a teacher - and which school wouldn't want a teacher like you?

The school where you teach is in a leafy area with well-to-do parents who value education. They work extensively with their children at home and fully support you. Should you need guidance or advice, just like during your student placements, experienced school teachers have adequate release time to coach you in your further professional development. You have a small class with experienced support staff who effectively meet any additional needs in your class and assist you in preparation of resources for exciting new learning. Your classroom is equipped with the latest technology, furniture and resources. The room is bright and spacious with many areas for children to learn in small groups or individually. As for children, you couldn't have hoped for a better prepared group. They speak, read and write well on entry to your class - your challenge now is to widen their curricular experiences and to create opportunities to apply the learned skills and knowledge. Your pupils have had superb pre-school experiences and easily follow your instructions. They work, listen, play and learn just as you would expect them to. The children can express themselves very well. They speak eloquently using a vast vocabulary bank. They are also very independent and eager to learn. You focus on teaching, as you should, enjoy watching your children making outstanding progress and achieving well above their peers elsewhere. Children in your class have high expectations of themselves and always seem to know what they have to do. You feel as if you were born to be a teacher and love every moment of it. Your lessons, days and terms flow with ease as all the basics are in place for you.

This book is for the rest of us.

A MATTER OF SKILL

A fancy name for the effective classroom routines is organisational skills. You can often hear the simple phrase good organisational skills being widely used in education. The phrase means the ability to fulfil tasks successfully. The skills themselves, however, are anything but simple in their impact – without them, you cannot function efficiently, whether as a class teacher or a school leader.

The greater your organisational skills, the greater your chances of success in making the impact on children in your care. To teach effectively and maintain healthy work-life balance, you must first develop and then continue to hone the skills that help you do your job well. Stress in teaching is often exacerbated by poor organisation and the skill of separating work and personal life is possibly the greatest protective factor for the modern teacher like you.

Note the repetition of the word skills rather than gifts. Being skills, they can be learned. This book will help you to learn them if you are new to teaching or assist you in refining the skills you already have if you are an experienced teacher.

MAKING THIS BOOK WORK FOR YOU

No matter how you approach this book – whether as a systematic course book, or as a reference book (we ourselves vary on this one) – it should sharpen your ability to organise your classroom routines, improve the impact of your teaching, develop independent pupils and progressively reduce your workload. While mastering effective classroom routines may appear to come naturally to some teachers, in reality it will take continuous reflection, evaluation and bringing about incremental improvements into your daily practice.

A word about the recommendations in this book. To be practical and realistic, we reviewed the most common school practices and described the effective routines we have either practised ourselves or those we observed in the most successful classrooms. The examples offered here are designed to give you a flavour of what it might look like in your classroom practice. They are recommendations only which serve as practical illustrations to help you understand the principles underpinning the classroom processes. You may use them to evaluate your own practice, adjust them to suit your needs or adopt them as they are.

TEACHING CLASSROOM ROUTINES

Education is not preparation for life; education is life itself.

JOHN DEWEY

The best routines are clear routines, and clear routines are for the most part simple routines. It means that they have to be simple enough to be explained, understood, taught and followed by all children and adults. The teacher, whose routines stand on those days when other staff cover the class, most certainly has devised them wisely and taught them well.

You will require many routines to operate effectively and efficiently as a teacher. This book offers you a range of techniques, for a range of occurrences: from lining up to class registration; from working on the carpet to dismissal at the end of the day.

In essence, the routines you establish will shape your

classroom climate. The spiral effect is remarkable. Have clear expectations, and your pupils become more responsible for their behaviour and learning. Similarly, as your powers of management and organisation increase, so does the level of job satisfaction and the quality of balance between your work and life.

MODEL WHAT YOU EXPECT

Always be clear what you expect and use modelling to assist you with that. It is a powerful and simple way which will help your pupils understand and practise your expectations. Once you have decided on what you want, be clear how and when you want it done. And, refrain from talking too much when explaining it to the children. Use this basic rule: if you want children to understand you, say it in such a way that they can repeat it.

When deciding on the routines, make sure your pupils are able to meet your expectations most of the time. Establish what your children are able to do and build incrementally upon the skills they already have. Raise your expectations progressively as children become more proficient in their ability to follow them. Gradually, adjust your routines to your teaching and your children's learning styles. Having established the basic routines, improve them as children go through the year so that what you expect of the pupils in the summer term is much higher than the expectations set for them in autumn. If your children are to be successful in meeting your expectations, make sure that those expectations are appropriate for their age and ability. For example, a nursery child unpegging their own painting and putting it on the drying rack is as laudable as a year 5 classroom running a guided reading carousel without teacher direction. Some successful examples are listed for you below. Below you will find some successful examples we have either implemented or observed. These examples are supplemented with advice we wished at times we had heard a little earlier in our teaching careers.

Model as appropriate and teach the pupils you have. Do not be that teacher fighting what the pupils should do at their age, stating what is unsuccessfully happening before you or firing off rhetorical questions. Start with what you have and shape it into what you want. If a routine slides, or, if you return after a weekend to find pupils having forgotten a basic routine they were able to do a few days before - pause. Stop the activity, focus the children's attention and model your expectations again. It would be easy to have little jugs to receive information, pouring in a little bit of knowledge each day and watching them fill until they reach the required level. But children are not jugs. They will have developmental leaps, at times stall and occasionally forget things entirely until prompted. Good teachers are also patient teachers - they never give up. To avoid frustration creeping into your practice, just remember how much you enjoy the days when together you suddenly exceed expectations and when you witness the joy of a child's delight at suddenly beginning to make the first steps at these moments.

Whatever expectations you set, you will **need to have visual reinforcement aides displayed around your room** to remind the children of those expectations. One thing that can be said about the displays is this - use them wisely. Select a prominent area in the room and use it to aid organisation. To help the pupils who are learning to read, use small laminated images stuck to walls or desks to show the stages of routines. Use this approach for all essential routines at the early stages of their implementation. For example, in the nursery you can display a set of small laminated images above the sink demonstrating the procedure for washing hands. It may consist of the following stages: run the water, put soap on the hands, rub the hands, rinse off the soap, close the tap and then dry the hands.

For pupils with SEND, place laminated timetables and instructions of procedures on their desks or walls at their stations. Some of your pupils may require support in starting work. One way to help them to be independent is by using prompt cards. A simple set may look like this:

1. Write the date and the title

2. Read the questions

3. Write the answers in your book

4. Ask your partner if you need help

The set of such written prompts may need to be supplemented with pictorial aids for some pupils. You can find online many simple graphics which will assist you with most of your needs.

Never presume anything when it comes to setting expectations. Explain what you mean by being quiet, sensible, tidy or smart looking. For example, show the tidy desk to the children.

Show them how to tidy up together as a team. Explain what each person should do and how to work collaboratively. Show where to put books, pencils, trays or any other items that need to be put away. Explain also what to do when something is broken or missing.

During these demonstrations, use clear directions. Make sure children understand what you want them to do - *Put your pencils in the tray* or *Place all Maths books in the red box*. Avoid non-specific remarks such as *You need to do better than that* or *Sit nicely*. Verbal directions such as *If you are on the red circle, I would like you to take your reading books to Mrs T.* or *Children in the reading corner, go the writing table please* aid faster transition times in class and help you avoid the slippery path of calling individual names as pupils lose attention. In a moment of feeling overloaded or overwhelmed, most children will latch on to the solution of making things better and feeling better when it's simply provided. At the start of the year, don't presume that your pupils enter the classroom with a shared expectation and knowledge of being tidy and sensible. Take them on the journey of improvement and recognise their progress from all starting points with praise.

In your classroom, you will set and model the expectations of many aspects related to children's learning and conduct. Below are a few examples you will need to demonstrate in your classroom.

When it comes to demonstrating the standards you expect in books, share how you expect the work to be laid out and presented. Show your children how to record the date, how to have sufficient space between words and what standard of handwriting you expect in their books. Teach them to use sharp pencils for neat presentation. Photocopy and display the examples of work which meet your expectations. Draw children's attention to them each time you need to remind them what you expect.

Model how children can do their independent work in different ways, not just sitting at a desk working in their books. Show them how to work collaboratively to solve problems, how to seek different solutions to problems using the resources at hand and not relying on the teacher. Encourage and teach them how to continue working at home with what has been started at school and how to persevere to achieve them best outcomes.

And do not expect silence in your lessons at all times. Demonstrate to children the appropriate ways of talking when working with others on the carpet, at the desks, at the play area or when tidying up. These skills can be taught very effectively through role play with younger children or rehearsals with older pupils.

To handle significant or regular playground difficulties, address them promptly. For example, spend some time on the playground watching your children play. You may notice the early signs of potential troubles and address them before they become problems spilling into the classroom or beyond. It is worth finding time to model solutions to prevent or deal with most social difficulties in the future.

Children learn differently and one of the most effective

ways of teaching them is through the role play. You can do it in this way: In small groups, guide children to act out very similar scenarios to those where they found difficult to manage. Help them, through acting, to find ways to resolve the difficulties. A later start to a lesson on the odd occasion will save much more learning time managing emotions or poor focus during the lesson.

Model how to speak to each other, how to show respect and take turns. Demonstrate how to ask questions and talk politely in class and on the playground. Model routinely to children how you use your indoor voice and the room will be a space of calm. Older children may benefit from noise thermometers - there are plenty of these shared online. An adult pointing to *talk to partners only*, *group table work* or *silent independent work* are very efficient ways of directing children without further adding to the disruption of learning for those who are focused on their work.

To help children become independent learners, make sure your **resources are labelled** and children can access them. Encourage children to use them during the lessons. Teach them how to independently access the resources, select the appropriate ones and be responsible at putting them away at the end. Model how to keep the resource areas tidy and safe. Move around the classroom as you are demonstrating it - pick up a dictionary and put it in the correct place. Now, ask one of your pupils to show how to do it and then practise with the whole class.

At the start of the year, or whenever the new pupils join

your class, show children where water fountains, medical room, library, ICT suite and the lost property areas are. Have a routine to take the new children around the school showing those places to them – this can be done by two of your pupils. Remember to explain the roles of different adults in school and who the children should go to. Take your children to see and introduce those adults to them. Finish the walk with time for questions you may not have anticipated, such as a fearful *…but what if I'm in the toilet when the fire alarm goes off?*

Never underestimate how a clear role or an appropriate direction can transform the pupils seemingly most reluctant to engage. Confidence and sense of security in us all grow from a feeling of capability and a sense of worth. Children are also guided by these basic principles even though they may not always be able to articulate or understand them.

PRACTISE WITH PUPILS

Pupils usually need some time to learn how to carry out certain routines. Once they have learned them, keep your expectations of quality and consistency high. Aim to keep to the minimum the need to remind children what you expect them to do. And, like with learning, differentiate your expectations depending on the pupils' abilities and the stage of their development. For example, you could adjust your expectations of the pupils who are new to English because they may not understand fully your requirements or instructions. Similarly, your expectation of the standard of work and its presentation will be different for children who are at different stages in their learning. In early years, for instance, it would be reasonable to have higher expectations of the autumn born children compared to the summer born pupils. Be wary of this presumption though as not all children follow this rule.

Your children will learn best if the practice is fun, fast-paced and the experience is positive for them. Knowing the needs and interests of your children will help you to achieve it. Here are some examples of how it may look like in practice:

If you need to model lining up, greeting another person, or some other routine, take a few minutes to quickly practise with pupils what you expect them to do during those routines. Encourage different desks to compete as they practise the routines. Go around and point out what exactly each desk does well. It will reinforce the behaviours you are trying to instil and bring in competition and fun. You can draw on the spirit of competitiveness in them by using a stopwatch. Cheer up the children as they go through each step of the process. Search online - there are many countdown timers to use on the classroom interactive boards with a variety of fun conclusions from popping balloons to fireworks animations.

Many of your routine will be easy to teach. The rest, on the other hand, will be quite complex and not so straightforward to implement. In such cases, simplify the more complex routines initially and train your children to carry out the simpler versions of those routines. When you notice that the children are ready, gradually increase the complexity of the routines as you go through the year.

Another way of implementing complex routines is by breaking them into small steps and practising each step separately. Stop the class after each step and allow all children to complete it before moving on to the next step. For instance, if pupils find transition from the desks to the carpet difficult, direct them first to tidy up their desks. Once this stage has been completed by all, ask children to stand up, push in their chairs and stand behind them. After that, direct the class to sit down on the carpet. If you want to teach your class can settle down on the carpet in an orderly manner, this transition can be done by selecting the groups of children from the desks that are ready. Direct one group at the time to move to the carpet and prepare for the next part of the lesson.

REINFORCE SUCCESS

Use simple and specific direct language to reinforce the routines children do well or in which they are progressing rapidly towards the expectations you have set. In your feedback to children, look for improvements rather than the perfect match of what they have accomplished to the expectations you have set. As children learn the classroom routines, offer your constructive feedback to them. Be specific in your comments – recognise the accomplishments of individuals and point out what exactly they do well: Well done, Andrew, for putting your books away before going to the carpet. Use your class reward system, if appropriate, and celebrate individual or group successes. Positive feedback from you will motivate your pupils to succeed. Being constructive, your feedback will guide those who the feedback is directed towards. It will also be of help to the other children - those who are just listening. They will hear and see what you are looking for and the next time they will do it too.

Children mature differently. They also seek attention in different ways. Be mindful of the children who may not yet have the maturity to get your attention appropriately. Occasionally, they will resort to the use of inappropriate ways to seek your reaction. They will do it either because that is what they have learned elsewhere or they may copy others. Sometimes, they will try as many different ways as they can possibly think of just to have you come, look or talk to them. The first thing to do in situations like this is to teach children how to get your attention in the correct way. If you do need to redirect a child, use a simple phrase stating what you want the child to do. Repeat it with minimal eye contact or emotion. Save your biggest reactions for praise. Your decision about the way to handle the situation will depend on the circumstances and the child. Note though that sometimes it can be more disruptive to address low-level misbehaviour instantly than it is to ignore it. A good way to handle it would be to move the child away from a potential audience and calmly discuss it there.

Children will try to please you and they will want to know if they are doing the right things. Draw their attention when noting the positive achievements by smiling and using a clear loud voice. Notice the small first steps of children who have found it hardest to regulate themselves in the classroom. Share their achievements with others. With the focus on positive aspects of behaviour and learning, your classroom will gradually become the environment in which children seek the opportunities to do the right things knowing that you will notice and reward them.

MODIFY

Having high expectations is important, but so is recognising individual needs. Occasionally, you may need to modify your expectations for some of your pupils. Here is one example when you may need to do it.

Ordinarily, you would expect children to make eye contact when talking or listening to others. Some children though may not be ready for this - either because of their specific needs, for example pupils with autism, or because making an eye contact is considered inappropriate in their culture. Whatever the reason, modify your expectations as appropriate. For instance, you can teach a child to look toward the person or a group – just over their eye level - when speaking to them. Be sure to explain to your class why you might occasionally need to modify the rules for some pupils. Children are sensitive to being treated fairly and want the rules to be applied consistently. Help them to understand the reasons and they will accept the modified approaches.

From the beginning, be clear what your expectations are. If it is necessary to break them down into stages, say so. Tell the children when you expect them to meet certain expectations. They will do better knowing what is coming next and when they are expected to master it by.

USE VISUAL AND AUDIO SIGNALS

Pupils respond well to a calm and confident manner in which the teacher sends a signal. The signal you send can be auditory, visual or a combination of both (for example clapping of the hands). In a busy learning environment, the use of visual signals is more likely to get your pupils' attention than trying to speak over their voices. So, get their attention first and before you speak, wait until everyone is paying attention and only then start addressing the children. Very soon, this waiting time will decrease and the pupils will learn to settle down, face you and listen within a very short period of time. Use the signals consistently as a clear message that you expect everyone to pay attention, listen and learn. Here are some examples how to use them.

Suppose your pupils are sitting on the carpet facing you. They will respond quickly to a visual gesture such as a raised hand or when you place an index finger on your lips and sit up straight. Children will first copy you and then copy each other which will speed up the message across the class. After a week of practising it, you should expect the class to settle down within 5-10 seconds although it depends on the age of the children. Younger children may need a bit longer to practise it, especially those with no prior school experience. While putting a finger on the lips would be appropriate for the children under the age of seven, a raised hand can be a better alternative for older pupils. A silent Simon says series of actions can be good for pupils who are not yet able to focus on more than one action at a time. Touch your nose, ears and so on slowly until the whole class is copying you. Sit and fold your arms as the last gesture. There is power in silence or the use of a soft tone to promote listening once attention is secured.

You may need to use an auditory signal when not all pupils can see you. Such situation can occur for example when children work independently at their desks. For that, establish a routine for drawing pupils' attention. One way to do it is to count: *5, 4, 3, 2, 1 - eyes on me*. Expect everyone in class to know that when they hear you count, they need to stop, turn towards you and listen. If children hold pens or any other objects, expect children to put them down. **Raise your hand and count on your fingers.** It will reinforce the message visually for those children who are looking at you and help those who are not facing you to notice it when they look at others. Do not rush through the counting though and give children enough time to settle down. Be sure to explicitly teach the pupils what you expect when you are counting. Repeat your expectations as you count down if necessary. Here is how you can do it.

As you count down, remind children what you expect them to do: *Five, stop writing and turn towards me; four, stop talking; three, put down your pencils…* Alternatively, if you are blessed with the confidence and a good singing voice, search online for a suitable tidy up time song you can enjoy with your class.

Your pupils can be in different places across the room and you may need to practise a variety of scenarios during which they need to listen to you from the places where they are at that moment. Once you have secured children's attention, you may need to follow it with the instructions such as to line up, to return to their desks or to come to the carpet. Watch how children perform these routines and call out the names of those who are doing the right things. Remember to point out what they do well and praise them: *Well done, Alice! Two team points for picking up toys and putting them into the correct basket.* You will notice how others will try to emulate the behaviour you have praised and will follow the routines you expect.

For tidying up at the end of activities such as Art, stop the class first. Make the children face you and quickly assign tasks to a selected group of pupils. Decide what needs to be done in the classroom and allow enough time for those activities. Be aware of the children's needs as you do so - those chosen to clear under the tables need to resist the urge to race through the tunnel network before them.

Instruct your children that once they have completed the assigned task, they must sit on the carpet or at their desks whichever is more appropriate. Certain tasks are more time consuming than others due to the nature of the task and because some children are faster than their peers.

You may not need all children to be involved in tidying the classroom. Guide those children who are not involved in tidying to engage in suitable activities; those who tidy up need to join these activities once they have completed their tasks. Such activities may involve opportunities for additional practice in spellings or times tables or reading the library books. With time, you will aim to instil the sense of responsibility and independence so that the children will utilise every minute of spare time independently. Expect the older children to self-direct in the choice of learning activities during those times.

Throughout the day, children will be watching for some signs from you to be certain that they are doing the right things. Teach them simple non-verbal cues to expect from you such as a nod or a thumb up to show your approval, a raised index finger to indicate that the pupil needs to be more attentive or a sideways moving index finger to show that the pupil needs to stop the wrong thing and follow the expectations. Eye gaze is also a very intuitive direction for most pupils. They will naturally look where you are silently focusing.

Your classroom routines are there to help you teach and your pupils to learn. The effectiveness of your routines therefore should be measured against this benchmark. If they do the job well, keep them. If they fail to offer that assistance to you or your children, be quick to change them. There is no reason why you should be carrying out any activity, no matter how smoothly it runs, unless it offers significant benefits to you and all of your children.

A well-designed and implemented set of key routines is one of the essential things that will contribute to your successful teaching career. So, it is important to make sure that you start off your day on the right foot.

ROUTINES AT THE START OF THE DAY

Success is no accident. It is hard work, perseverance, learning, studying, sacrifice and most of all, love of what you are doing or learning to do.

PELE

The main thing to be said about the start of the day is this: Keep it highly structured and predictable. If you are in doubt about what routines to review or implement, start with the activities you currently carry out in your daily practice. Some of the examples could be: entering the classroom, settling on the carpet, taking the registers or early morning work. Start with a small number of the essential routines and expand it as your children become ready for the next step. It is only natural to introduce the simple routines first and then increase their complexity gradually once the children have mastered the basics.

First, decide which of the early morning routines will better help you to achieve what you want. As a start, list some of the activities you are already doing every morning and jot down any improvement ideas that come to your mind. Read them through: it will probably generate further ideas, which you can jot down too. Study them, noting similarities and consistency in your approach. Shift about these various ideas until the best workable approach emerges. But remember: a routine delivers when it is carefully planned and craftily executed.

Here are some specific examples of general morning routines and detailed hints that will help.

ENTERING THE CLASSROOM

All children should enter the classroom ready to learn. To speed up the transition and reduce the wasted time to a minimum, introduce clear steps into the process, so that it follows a certain structure. For instance, it may consist of the following stages:

1. Lining up

2. Walking through the school

3. Putting away belongings

4. Settling down to learn

Below are the detailed descriptions of routines for each of these stages.

LINING UP

When lining up pupils at the start of the day, ensure that you are on the playground, or at your door if children enter directly into your classroom, before the bell goes off. When the bell rings, position yourself in front of the children who should be in line. Playground tends to be noisy in the morning, so, to help your pupils follow your instructions, use visual signals such as a raised hand, a finger over your lips or a combination of both. After successful training and practice, children should follow your routine by watching you, repeating your gestures and lining up quietly within a week or two.

Teach your children to line up in two parallel lines so that you can give verbal instructions when necessary without having to raise your voice for those at the back to hear you. Walk along the line recognising good examples of lining up and rewarding children for successfully meeting the expectations you have set. Use the reward system that you have in your class and school such as team points, marbles or stickers to recognise and promote the behaviours and attitudes you wish to instil. As you inspect the line, ensure that children look smart - for example that their shirts are tucked in - and ready to enter the school. Enter the school when all children are ready.

WALKING THROUGH THE SCHOOL

On the face of it, walking through the school is simple. All you have to do is go through the corridors at the head of the line and expect the children to follow you.

But there is more to it than that. The pace at which you walk, the behaviour in the line as you proceed and the impact of the other children or adults walking across the school at the same time as your class all require careful consideration and observation on your part.

Move at the speed which will allow your children to follow you. It should be not too pacey, as in this case children begin to run to catch up with you, nor too slow causing disruptive congestion in the line during which behaviour begins to deteriorate and children start to talk or argue. If the journey to your classroom is long, or the corridor has turns, decide at which points you want to stop waiting for the whole class to catch up. Wait for the children to form a neat line again, calm down and then proceed further. This procedure may be necessary to perform a few times depending on the length and complexity of the route. Use the same approach when you take the class on trips. By following these simple steps, you will always ensure that your line arrangement retains its order, you have a good oversight of your class and children move safely.

As you move across the school, walk along the line and direct the children at the front to the point where they need to stop and wait for further instructions. Such stopping points can be at the corridor turns or at the sets of internal doors. The last such point should be just before your classroom door where you can make sure that the children are calm and quiet before they enter the room. At this point you may consider having your class line up in a single file line to make the entrance into the classroom more manageable.

PUTTING AWAY BELONGINGS

As always, be clear and keep to the point when instructing the children about the routines on how to put away their bags, coats or water bottles.

When the whole class enters the room at the same time and your class coat pegs are located in the same area, it will inevitably lead to children being at best in a congested and at worst in an unsafe place. You can combine the need for the speedy and safe process of classroom entry by directing groups of children to carry out different activities as they enter. You need to split the class into groups – these can be your usual table groups - and direct each group to different locations. It means that the group which is trying to hang up their coats on the pegs is unlikely to be at the same location with a group which has been directed to put their school bags in their draws. Yet another group of children could be placing their homework into the tray. When these activities have been thought through well, and the furniture arrangements reflect your intent to streamline the process, you can organise the classroom entry into a very efficient procedure resulting in a smooth and calm transition.

Arrange a suitable location for your draws by having them placed away from the coat pegs. Plan your classroom furniture arrangements carefully by allocating the draws and the coat pegs in such a way that pupils will be spread out when accessing them at the same time. One way to do it is to place the sets of draws against different walls in your classroom or to space them out leaving enough room between them for the two groups not to impede on each other's space.

You can arrange a smooth and efficient process using these simple steps. Divide your children into groups and instruct them where to go each time they enter the class in the morning. You can do it by teaching them the order of activities for each group. A simple arrangement of this procedure is illustrated below.

	Coat pegs	Sets of draws	Homework tray
Step 1	Green table	Orange table	Red table
Step 2	Red table	Green table	Orange table
Step 3	Orange table	Red table	Green table

In the example above, you can teach the Green table to put their coats on the pegs first while the Orange table can go to the draws to place their bags or water bottles there. At the same time, the children from the Red table can proceed to the homework tray to place their homework. The groups then rotate through the remaining two activities – different children will do it at different speeds but the overall flow of change will remain stable.

When you decide to teach children how to proceed through these stages, teach one group at the time in the order they need to enter the classroom and move through these steps in the correct order. Once the pupils have completed the first part of the process, i.e. have hung their coats or put their book bags in their draws, they will need to proceed to the second and then third parts. Using this straightforward approach, you will ensure that the whole process of classroom entry in the morning is smooth, quick and safe.

Note that, as with any other routine you introduce to your class, you should explain what it is for, model how to execute it correctly and practise with your pupils until they learn the habit of doing it each time they enter your room.

SETTLING DOWN

Having completed the initial start of the day routines – lining up, walking into the classroom and putting coats and bags away – children now need to settle down at their desks or on the carpet ready to learn.

For the very young children – those in early years, year one and two - the usual place to settle down first thing in the morning is on the carpet. Many activities, sometimes simultaneously, take place during this part of the day – you greet your children, introduce them to what you have planned for the day, ask them questions, praise for the previous day's achievements and assign the responsibilities for the day. As pupils get older, they are less likely to be on the carpet and therefore will go directly to their desks in the morning.

Within two to four minutes, depending on the children's age and the degree to which the routines have been imbedded, you should expect your class to be settled and ready. You can now start your registration routine continuing to ensure that every minute of the morning is put to good use.

REGISTRATION

There are two basic ways to do the registration of the class – with the registration being the main activity in which all children are expected to participate until the process is over, and the registration being an activity which runs in the background of another process during which the pupils are engaged in learning activities. It seems prudent to deploy the latter approach since it allows for a lot of valuable time to be used for learning during the registration process.

ACTIVITIES DURING THE REGISTRATION

As children begin to settle down on the carpet or at their desks, and then for the rest of the registration process, engage those who have already settled down in meaningful learning activities. The activities should not require an adult to lead them - you should not extensively plan for them either. Examples may include learning the times tables or spellings, practising handwriting or checking and following up on your marking and feedback. With well-established routines, children will learn to engage in these activities with minimum input from an adult. If you have an additional adult in your classroom, consider delegating this responsibility to this person. An experienced teaching assistant can prove to be very capable of overseeing the settling in process. It means that you can continue your preparations for the registration or work with individual children during that time. A few examples of activities during the settling in process are described below.

If you expect your children to settle down on the carpet, display an activity of the board which they can follow and participate in either independently or as a class. A simple example of the morning activity for the nursery children can be playing a familiar nursery rhyme to reinforce children's counting skills. For older children, it can be a list of spellings or new vocabulary, a short news passage with follow up questions, a thought-provoking statement or a dilemma with a few questions to reflect on.

You can bring in a creative touch into this part too. Create a calm working atmosphere by putting on quiet relaxing music to play in the background. Children will respond well to it and calm down quickly after coming in from the noisy and active playground.

FIRE REGISTERS

Some of the daily activities expected to be carried out by the class teacher allow little or no flexibility for the class teacher. Fire register, together with attendance registration, are two examples of such activities – they must be done first thing in the morning and after lunch.

Some schools may have electronic systems in place and there may be no need to duplicate the process – the attendance register also serves the purpose of being the fire register. Other schools, nevertheless, register pupils using paper registration forms.

The process of fire registration should be no different to that carried out for attendance - pupils should be engaged in learning activities while you carry out the registration. Having taken the register, you may need to send it to the office. For that, assign this role to pupils. It should be sufficient to send one pupil although younger children or those with additional needs may need to be partnered with another child.

A word about the fire evacuation procedures – practise them as soon as possible. Familiarise yourself and your children with the fire escape routes. You will need to make sure that your children know how to evacuate from the building in the event of emergency. From time to time, remind them of how to act during that time – they need to be calm when the fire alarm goes off, line up in the usual manner and leave the building quickly. It is wise to have regular(termly) training sessions with your class on how to exit the school building and line up at the assembly point.

DINNER REGISTERS

As with the previous two kinds of registration, you will take the dinner register in the morning. The arrangements for taking the dinner register should be the same as those for the attendance and fire registration. From time to time, your class will be out on trips or engaged in other activities which will last most of the school day. On these occasions, pupils will not be having their lunch the usual way in school. When planning these activities, inform the kitchen and the office in advance. Also, communicate to the parents to make provisions for children's packed lunches on those days.

With practice, you should complete all your registration processes within three to five minutes. During this time, you should expect all your children to be learning independently in a calm and orderly way.

MORNING PRAYER

Teachers are employed in all types of schools and an ample number of them are faith schools. If you work in a faith school, it is usually expected of you to lead the class prayer at the start of the day, before lunch time, after lunch and at the end of the day.

After the registration, ask your class to face the prayer corner. Consider having an object to focus on such as a candle. Allow time to calm down and focus. This is an opportunity for you to allocate the role to lead the class prayer to a pupil. The pupil can stand in front of the classroom facing the class and leading the class through the prayer. Initially, you will need to lead it with the pupil modelling how to prepare the class and how to speak clearly. With time, your class will know what to expect and this activity will be run by your designated pupils.

DAILY SCHEDULE

To help your pupils understand what will happen during the day, and to give yourself an opportunity to clarify what you expect of them, go through the events that will happen in class and school that day.

DISPLAYING THE SCHEDULE

Having prepared your daily schedule, you now need to put it to good use. Display it and point at the events as you go through them. During the day, adults and children will be able to refer to it as required. For young children, use picture cues placed next to the event titles to help children make sense of the words. For older pupils, display the start times of the events. They will use this activity as an opportunity to learn and practise the use of time in meaningful and practical ways. Have the start times separate from the event titles to give you flexibility to alter the order of events if necessary.

One of the ways to display and share the schedule is to use laminated picture cards of daily events alongside a few blank cards to write on. The cards can be removed when the activities or lesson are completed. They can be rearranged on the days with unexpected events. For older children, a list on the side of the whiteboard may be adequate.

Many of your daily events will be repeated on a regular basis. To cater for that, prepare cards with the regular event names. There are plenty of ready-made downloadable resources on the internet. You can choose the cards that are right for you and save a lot of time not having to create them yourself. Chose the right place for the daily schedule to make is easily visible and accessible. For example, you can display it at the front of the classroom close to the area where you are positioned when teaching the whole class.

SHARING THE SCHEDULE FOR THE DAY

Going through the schedule for the day with young children is part of the learning process through which they acquire a wide range of skills and knowledge. When children are settled on the carpet, ask volunteers to help you to go through the events for the day. You can read out the events card by card announcing their start times if these are displayed. Ask the child helper to hold the card showing it to the class. Contribute with the details of each event: At 9:00am we will have a Maths lesson where you will learn to add two numbers. After Maths, you will have a break time – remember to visit the school garden and check how the garden vegetables on your patch have changed. After the break, we will have a story time. Once you have completed discussing the event displayed on the card, ask your helper to place on the schedule. The child will then pick up and hold the next card. When going through the schedule with younger children, use this opportunity to improve their language skills. Ask questions such as: What comes before phonics? What is the first thing after lunch? What is the last thing we will do today?

After a few weeks of reviewing the schedule card by card,

you can post all cards on the schedule before the start of the day. The child helper then can point to the event cards as you discuss them. For the older children, many of the daily events will be self-explanatory and you will only need to go through the details of the events you wish to emphasise to them.

As with any activity, seek the feedback from your children. Create opportunities which would allow pupils to share their views and ideas. Children are more likely to engage positively in all learning you have planned for them if they have also taken part in planning for it. This in turn will benefit you too allowing you to know what works best for your class or individual pupils.

CLASS JOBS

Allocation of class jobs should be one of the first things of yours at the start of the year. Get it right at the beginning and you will engage your pupils as well as reduce your workload for the rest of the year.

There are three basic ways to job allocation: asking pupils to volunteer for jobs, assigning the jobs to pupils, and advertising available class jobs. Depending on the circumstances, the age of your children and the types of jobs, you can consider either one or a combination of two or three ways as appropriate.

Once you have allocate the jobs, make the process manageable by creating and displaying a *job chart* containing the job titles and the name of pupils responsible for them. Add the guidelines reminding your children what different tasks entail.

Try to include tips on how and when they are to be carried out for more complex jobs.

When going through the chart, which can be done during the discussion of the schedule for the day in the morning, identify the jobs that need to be covered due to pupil absences and assign those roles to others. Train older children to monitor the jobs chart independently and have sensible ways of agreeing on who would be substituting the absent pupils without having to involve you each time.

The chances are that at the start of the year you have listed more than one weekly class job. You might want to list the jobs together with the requirements and discuss them with your class as soon as possible. Explain which jobs you will be assigning on a weekly basis and which ones will be advertised. This process can create a valuable learning opportunity for your children. Plan a circle time and ask your children to share their views on the qualities that would be necessary for certain jobs. Include their ideas in the job specifications when you advertise the class jobs.

ASSIGNING CLASS JOBS

Keep the process of job assignment simple and short. Ask children to volunteer for odd jobs and allocate them yourself randomly. You can select children by pulling out a lolly stick with a name of a child (having a class set of lolly sticks with names of children can be useful in many other activities). Another way of assigning weekly jobs is by allocating them to groups or by going down your class list in a systematic order. This will ensure that you have some kind of a system that will offer fair chances for all.

ADVERTISING CLASS JOBS

One of the most important roles of education is to prepare children for life. Applying for an advertised class job gives them an opportunity to experience how to best present themselves to be successful at job interviews. Children will learn about the qualities potential employers might be looking for.

Here is an example of a job advert you may place:

Lunch helpers required for nursery class

We are looking for four KS2 pupils to assist for 15 minutes at lunch time (12:05pm to 12:20pm). The chosen applicants will be expected to encourage the nursery children to eat their lunch, help them safely cut up food and engage the nursery children in group games. You will need to be able to work as a team and have the ability to communicate effectively with young children showing patience, understanding and empathy. You must be committed to turning up for every shift.

Full details and the application forms can be obtained from Ms Green in the Nursery. At the end of the autumn term, you will be rewarded with cake and juice. At the end of the year, you will be paid with a book voucher.

Closing date: Friday 14th September 2018

Interviews: Tuesday 18th September 2018

Start: Monday 24th September 2018

Note that this advert allows older children to apply for a job in a different class during lunch time. You can also offer opportunities for older children to read to or with younger pupils. Similarly, you can advertise different types of class jobs.

TYPES OF CLASS JOBS

You will probably have to think carefully before you decide exactly which jobs you want to be given to your pupils, and which ones can be left for you to do. Start off by making a list at the start of the year. It should include simple routine activities which children can carry out well.

The following examples should give you a flavour of daily class duties that can be assigned to pupils.

Class registers

One or two pupils bring the registers at the start of the day and first thing after lunch. After the registration, they return them to the office.

Laptop or iPad trollies

If safe and appropriate, two pupils are assigned to take out the laptops or iPads for the lessons. At the end of the lesson, they are responsible for the collection and placement of all IT equipment back into the trollies.

Watering plants

During quiet times, such as upon the return from break, one child waters classroom plants and rotates them to be closer to the natural light.

Recording the weather charts

This activity is usually led by a teacher working with younger children. As class discuss the weather on the day, a child helper displays corresponding words or images on the class weather chart. Have children keep tally charts to keep track of weather patterns. Use these at the end of the month to create bar graphs, discuss, and analyse the collected data.

Looking after class pets

Two children feed and change water for the class pets. Regularly, they spend time cleaning and improving the pets' habitat. Offer health and safety training, suitable equipment such a gloves and water sprays. Display the exact instructions about the steps to be taken for this type of job and supervise the children initially. Change one helper mid-week and another one at the end of the week. In this way you will ensure that there will always be one child who has done the job for some time and can train the new helper.

Handing out and collecting books

To speed up the process, this activity can be carried out by three or four pupils. Divide the class into areas. Expect each helper to look after his or her designated area. The same helpers can give out and collect the resources when children work on the carpet.

As these examples show, it is possible to cover vast areas of classroom activities where you can help your pupils to become independent and responsible. Be creative and give your children a chance to surprise you by how responsible and reliable they can be.

EARLY MORNING WORK

Getting the right start to the day - that is always a challenge as children come to school. Starting with a variety of 5-10min early morning work tasks can be your solution. Try this approach - easing them gently into the right inquisitive and relaxed mood for learning. Experiment with various tasks until you settle on the selection that best balances all your competing needs.

The most typical use of early morning work is to practise

the work previously taught that might need to be consolidated. Your choice of work should depend on the outcomes you are aiming for – and driven by the needs of your class. Is it important to consolidate the previous day's work? If so, choose the work your children can do independently. Well-chosen activities will help them to internalise the taught concepts. Does their work not meet the expected standards yet? In this case, ask the children to go through your feedback in their books, compare their work to the expectations you have set and make improvements by editing the work.

Here are some guidelines to help you when setting early morning work.

CONSOLIDATING NEW LEARNING

Having completed teaching a lesson – new facts, concepts or skills – you now have to allow time for children to practise, independently or in groups, what you have taught them. As it happens, the time during the lessons is rarely enough to fully embed the new learning.

The purpose of the consolidation work in the morning is to allow enough time for your pupils to practise the new skills and apply the new knowledge in different contexts. They need to know not only how to do particular tasks but know what they are doing and why. More than that, they must have deep understanding of how to use the new learning in a variety of contexts. For this, plenty of practice is required and regular 5-10min sessions in the morning are often good times to help with that.

The activities for some children might consist of additional opportunities to practise the previous day's activities. You may have identified it through your assessment of the work in the children's books noticing that they make too many mistakes. Before you set this task, ask yourself whether the children make these mistakes having fully understood the concept you have taught in the lesson. If your answer is No, you should go straight to explaining the concept to them again. Only when you are confident that they understand it well, give them activities to practise new knowledge or skills independently.

For those pupils who have grasped the new skills, it is time for challenge. Task them to apply the skills in solving real life problems. Some of them may benefit from transferring the new skills into other areas of learning making connections across topics or subjects.

Here are some examples of early morning work tasks which can help to consolidate new learning in History and Geography.

Practice

- Name at least four oceans and all continents using a map, atlas and a globe to locate them.

- Name and locate major mountain ranges and rivers of the UK.

- Create a personal time line of the key events in your lifetime.

Challenge

- Explain how some of the topological features of regions have changed over time.

- Explain the importance of arts on the lives of people in Roman and Tudor times.

- Explain why different invaders might have had the need to raid other lands and how they did it.

Skills transfer

- Design a human colony and a suitable transport to settle on the Moon.

- Create a survival guide for a person from the Stone Age being transported into the modern day.

- Create a diary entry of a child in Dresden during its bombing by the Allied Air Forces.

Whichever subject area or level of challenge you choose, do keep adjusting your expectations, widening the skills set and making learning meaningful to the children. And always bear in mind two rules.

One: the activities are there to help your children to learn and understand something new - not to keep them busy. If they are not learning anything they don't know, change the activity to another one which can meet this requirement.

Two: display the quality of work you expect your children to produce and give them enough time to produce it. Show what you want their end product to look like and explain how to achieve it.

RESPONDING TO MARKING

With marking, as with any type of feedback, it is only of any use if the pupils have time to reflect on it and practise to improve following the teacher's guidance. Traditionally, teachers mark books after school so it is only the following day that children can see the feedback from them. It would be a waste of your time marking the books and then move on to the next lesson and new activities without offering an opportunity for your pupils to read, reflect and improve on your feedback.

Before setting the task of going through your marking, train the children what exactly you expect them to do. Model how to read and interpret your comments - avoid rushing and making your handwriting difficult for children to read. Tell the children what they should do with any suggestions for improvement you have made or the errors you have highlighted. Even if your comments are open ended questions, the choice for answers or follow up work is immense. Make sure that in responding to your marking, pupils maintain focus on the learning outcomes you expect them to achieve. Referring back to the success criteria is a good start – it is here that the children can self-evaluate how accurately they are meeting the expected outcomes, not you having to go over their responses again.

PEER SUPPORT WORK

Needless to say, the impact of peer-to-peer support depends largely on whether you teach your children how to do it or not. Relying on a teacher to be the sole educator is never a solution. Children need to be skilled in working with and learning from others.

Peer support activities are often set up by pairing up more able children with those who might benefit from additional input. First a word of warning. The peer support must not mean higher attaining pupils teaching lower attaining ones. Working in partnership with others is the same in mixed-ability groups as it is across the same ability groups. The difference, however, is not in what they do but how they work together. In peer support work, as in all quality learning, engagement and opportunity are the key.

Whether children work in similar or mixed-ability groups, train them to work collaboratively focusing on specific goals. These may be subject specific or wider learning goals such as ability to take turns, listen to others, use technical vocabulary or to demonstrate deep understanding and explain the meaning of certain concepts.

Suppose, for example, you would like your pupils to go over the weekly spellings during the early morning work. You are having problems with many pupils not spending enough time to learn spellings at home. You think they will benefit from practising at school. Your plan might look like this:

Children settle down at their desks or with their usual mixed-ability partner. They take turns in the *Look, Cover, Write, Check* spelling practice. They also describe, explain and say one sentence for each spelling word.

An added benefit of mixed-ability pairing is the exposure of lower attaining pupils to higher level vocabulary and modelling from the higher attaining partners.

Early morning work can prove to be an invaluable opportunity to engage children in many learning activities for which there is lack of time during the lessons or which the children cannot do at home. Remember though that some learning gaps or children's needs call for special handling, regardless of what tasks you have chosen. It means that you will have to plan additional teaching or specialist input to help those pupils.

HANDING IN HOMEWORK

Pupils' tour through the day is in some ways like a commuter's journey on a familiar route. Follow the usual path, and you will get to the destination. A routine is like a travel plan. It enables your pupils to carry out an activity smoothly and quickly.

- Handing in homework works smoothly if conducted according to a few rules:

- Have a tray for handing in homework. Children from the age of four can learn to do it independently.

- Allocate space for the homework tray along the traffic path where children arrive into your classroom. The tray should not be too close to the entrance door but somewhere between the coat pegs and children's draws if those are located along the same line. Once the children have hung their coats, and before they get to put away their bags, they need to take the homework out of their bags and place it into the homework tray.

- Have a recording sheet for children to put a tick against their names once they have handed in their homework. It will save a lot of your time administering record keeping.

- Some parents and children like doing extra work at home. Place a spare work tray next to the homework tray where children can select extra work to take home.

Bear in mind the time pupils may spend on this activity. It needs to be as brisk as hanging a coat or putting a bag in a draw. Avoid having them stand about the tray trying to locate the homework and thus keeping everyone else waiting in a line behind them. Also, make it clear that you do not expect children to hand in any additional homework they may choose to take.

COMMUNICATING WITH PARENTS

The good teacher knows that having harmonious relationships with parents is often the key to understanding the children and helping them thrive. To build the harmonious relationships with parents, you need to know how to communicate with them effectively.

Parents, just like you, are busy people. Having brought their child to school, they sometimes want to tell you that the child may not feel well that morning, that they forgot to bring the homework, or advise you of something else which they feel you may need to know. Apart from telling you something, parents may have some questions or would like you to explain something to them.

Dealing with many parents in the morning can be surprisingly difficult, particularly when as you are trying to collect the children from the playground. A brief chat in the morning is usually enough to sort out any queries or pass on any information to a parent. Try to be on the playground 5min before the bell rings. Your regular availability will send a positive message to the parents – you are there for them should they need you.

Letting parents know how well their children do in school is part of your job. And often, there is much positive to share with parents about their children. Nothing is more encouraging for a parent and a child than have your praise. These may be huge leaps or small improvements - they all make a big difference to both children and parents.

As with any private matters, call the parent and a child aside. Let them know what exactly you are pleased about – *Well done, Charlie, for passing your three times tables! You must have worked incredibly hard to learn them within a week*. Give encouragement *I look forward to seeing you work as hard every week.*

Be curious, ask how the child is getting on with work at home and what interests the child pursues. Showing your personal interest in the wellbeing of the child and trying to understand his or her needs is often the proof the parents look for to be reassured that you care about their child. Remember to ask them whether there is anything that they may find helpful. Guide them to the useful resources or services. It is easy to see how working together with parents the children can progress much faster in their academic, emotional and social development. Your work in the classroom also becomes easier as a result of the effective partnership you manage to establish with the parents of your children.

Occasionally, however, you may need to raise concerns with parents if the children underperform or their behaviour falls below the standards you expect. How then, do you deal with a small problem you wish to discuss with a parent?

The first step is to call a parent aside. Always be professional, confidential and specific. Don't put the problem down to child's behaviour or bad attitude. If the child's behaviour or standards of work are an issue, tell exactly what standards you expect and how precisely the child failed to meet these standards. Explain what the child needs to do to meet the expectations and how you can help. Listen to the parent and answer tactfully. Offer a longer meeting after school if necessary.

The matter is much trickier when you have dissatisfied parents. How, for example, can you deal with a parent whose child came home with paint on his or her clothes? Or, someone who wishes to know why their child's reading book has not been changed? Or, parents who wish to talk to you about children playing too roughly at lunch? With many dissatisfied parents, problems may begin to mount. The temptation is to try to avoid discussing them altogether. Some teachers try to turn a blind eye in these circumstances. They hope that matters will improve unaided, that it is temporary and the problem somehow will sort itself out. And in some cases, they may be lucky – the problem may indeed solve itself. But there is no guarantee that it will – and things may get worse. Remember that it is better to act early than late when a neglected problem turns into a crisis. The chances are, some of those problems can be dealt with on the playground while the other matters may need separate meetings or telephone conversations to be arranged.

LESSONS

The art of teaching is the art of assisting discovery.

MARK VAN DOREN

Every minute of your lesson is a minute of learning. At least, every minute should be used for that purpose. After all, your lessons - their parts and transitions between them – reflect on you as a teacher.

A well prepared lesson can help you cover all you have planned and utilise your time to focus on what matters most. Skilfully constructed parts that fit well and flow effortlessly can help your children get most from your lessons. The lessons you plan and teach represent an important part of what teaching is about. Make yours good.

This chapter gives advice on how to organise many routines that you need during your lessons – from specific activities to transitions between them.

CARPET TIME

The way you use your carpet space depends largely on your aims. Are you reading a story with children and need them to be close to you? Or are you teaching a small group while the rest of the children work independently at their desks? In any case, keep your mind open as to whether the carpet, the desks or the use of both best serve the needs of your class.

ALLOCATING CARPET SPACES

The important thing to bear in mind when settling down children on the carpet is that it has to take as little time as possible. Neither you nor your children should be waiting pointlessly for the session to start.

As a rule, you decide where exactly each child should sit on the carpet before you start the new academic year. Hence the need for certain prior information about the class to help you make that decision. What are the children's individual needs? Which children focus or can see best by sitting near the front? Who needs to be supported on the carpet by the teacher or a teaching assistant? The trouble is, these questions are easy to answer when you know the class. When taking a new class, the best procedure is this: speak to the previous class teacher. If you work in the same school, arrange the end of summer transition meeting when you know which class you take.

But, what if you are new to the school or you are a Reception class teacher whose children are new to the school? A good rule in both cases is to leave that decision until later when you get to observe the children and speak to their parents. In the meantime, make an interim seating plan based on the information you have.

Whatever you do, tell your class from the start that the sitting plan is temporary and you will be making adjustments as you get to know the children better. They will expect changes and, when those changes do come, you will be able to implement them smoothly.

SETTLING DOWN ON THE CARPET

Suppose your class are entering the room and you would like them to go straight to the carpet. The arrangements in this case are quite clear. Providing the path to the carpet from the door is wide enough, all children should follow the same path and settle down on the carpet. Notice the impact of the order in which your children line up and where they sit on the carpet. If the entry point to the carpet area is at the back of the carpet space – at the furthest point away from the board - you need those children who are at the front of the line to sit at the front of the carpet. Arranging your lining up order in this way, will help you avoid having the rest of the class to walk across the carpet stepping between those who are already sitting on it. Likewise, make similar deliberations if the path to the carpet is from the side. You need to make the necessary decisions regarding these arrangements before the start of the year at the time when you decide on the lining up order, the location of the coat pegs, distribution of children's trays, the seating plan and the carpet space allocations.

As the children begin to settle down on the carpet, a part of your class will be in the classroom while others will still be in the corridor. So, the best way for you to position yourself is near the door. Here, you will be able to see all children and direct them if necessary. If you have a teaching assistant, he or she can engage with the children who are already on the carpet. The adults' roles can be exchanged depending on the needs or activities. As with registration, when settling down on the carpet you can put a short activity on the board for those who are already sitting or still entering.

A hallmark of any high quality process involving children is that learning always takes place. Put yourself into pupils' place. Would you find it more productive if there was a simple stimulating activity to be engaged with while you are waiting for others to settle? One useful and simple tip to help improve this routine is to display a thought-provoking question on the board: Which five words would describe your best qualities? What makes you special? Pushing boundaries – a virtue or a vice? Once the pupils have settled on the carpet, and before you start the next activity, ask one or two children to share their reflections. Ability to speak well expressing opinions, challenging status quo or taking into consideration the views of others is one of the key skills the children need to master to be successful in life. These seemingly simple moments on the carpet make a great deal of difference in your children's development. They are examples of quality teaching which appears to come naturally to the experienced high calibre teachers yet in reality requires careful planning and skilful execution.

In nursery or reception, you may have a set up where parents can bring children into the room. In this case, plan a free flow time when children visit the play areas of their choice where the resources and activities have been set up for them. They can play there until the teacher is ready to call them to the carpet. If the children go directly to the carpet, consider playing the nursery rhyme during the settling down process. Either you or the nursery nurse can lead the signing. At times, when an adult leads a story reading session, allow children who arrive early to collect a book from a box to take to the carpet if the entry routines in your school are likely to extend the registration period. As selection of books which would allow active participation full of movement, a good example can be *'We're Going on a Bear Hunt'*, will help you achieve good engagement and avoid distraction from the children who arrive late.

In other scenarios for moving to the carpet – such as moving from the desks or play areas – try the following systematic set of guidelines. They should help you achieve the same goals.

MOVING FROM DESKS TO THE CARPET

For straightforward tasks – such as moving the whole class or a group from the desks to the carpet – the best advice is simply: ask all children to stand up, to move their chairs in and to sit down on the carpet. Initially, when you teach them this routine, do one step at the time though. Also, you may decide that it is easier to manage the transition if you direct one group at the time to move to the carpet. After practising for some time, you will notice that the children are ready to move to the carpet - the whole at once.

MOVING FROM PLAY AREAS

In early years, moving the whole class from play areas to the carpet is lengthier and more intricate. Children are usually spread over the large area and are engaged in play. It often means that before they can move to the carpet the children need to tidy up first. This is a more challenging routine for children of that age so you will need to allow some time for them to learn it.

At the play areas, where the children are usually engrossed in activities, the noise level and children's attention to what they are doing is be a barrier you need to overcome. Your first task is to get their attention. Use your usual way of getting children's attention at this point – they need consistency in order to respond without delay. You can use a chime, small bell or clapping a simple tune – whichever is more appropriate as your choice may depend on the noise level or the size of the area over which the children are spread. Or, you may say something like this: *Class. Stop and face me*. At this point, you should expect every child to stop playing or talking and turn towards you. The additional adult in your class should be helping you by attending to the areas where the children are still playing or not facing you. One effective way to engage the children is to ask them to raise both their hands or place their hands on their heads. Train your additional adult quietly guide the children, using both verbal and visual cues, to follow your instruction. Speak when all children are quiet, facing you and paying attention: *Tidy up and come to the carpet.* Consider allocating the tidying up of different areas to different groups of children: *Sharks - tidy up the construction area. Whales – tidy up the home corner. When your area is tidy, come to the carpet and sit down in a circle.*

Some of your children may be using outdoor play areas. In this case, position yourself at the door when guiding the children what to do. If you have an additional adult in your classroom, this person can oversee the process of tidying up outside and the transition of children to the carpet from there.

For those children who have finished tidying up and have settled on the carpet, an adult can lead activities such as signing a nursery rhyme or counting. Alternatively, play calm music and ask children to close their eyes trying to imagine what is happening in a story played by the music – you will have to teach them how to do it first. By the end of the first term in school, you should expect children to tidy up and settle down on the carpet within three minutes.

Another simple technique to use during the whole class transitions to the carpet is to display a countdown timer on the board. Alternatively, hold up your hand and count on your fingers. Pupils' attention and focus vary depending on their age and needs. Using verbal and visual stimuli will help and speed up the transition.

DISMISSING CHILDREN FROM THE CARPET

Once you have completed your carpet session, children will need to be dismissed from the carpet – back to their desks, to line up or straight outside to the playground.

Before sending children back to the desks, first decide whether it is better to do it group by group or as the whole class. Initially, when children learn this routine, sending children one group at the time is more likely to meet your expectation of orderly and smooth transition. Also, it will provide you with opportunities to guide and commend each group as they do it.

If children sit in rows, send one row at a time. Start from the front so the rest of the class can see them as they do it. Whenever possible, give feedback focusing on the positive aspects of leaving the carpet. Emphasise what is right, rather than what is not. Use factual language. Be sparing of superlatives or exaggerated expressions.

As always, engage those who have successfully completed the transition. If they are at the desks, they should start their work. If they are waiting in a line, direct them to go over a specific display work in the classroom and recap on particular learning aspects. Then, when the whole class is in the line, follow up with a few questions related to the task before taking the class out.

INDIVIDUAL WHITEBOARDS

Individual whiteboards are items that many teachers like to avoid. Children tend to doodle on them instead of doing work or play and not pay attention to the teacher. Time taken to replace dried out pens, give out the whiteboards and put them away eats into the lesson. The often-confined carpet space may cause difficulties for children and have a negative impact on their behaviour. Despite all these reservations, with careful planning and managed approach the whiteboards can prove to be an invaluable and a versatile classroom resource for you and your children.

This section is designed to provide you with the tools that make the use of the whiteboards less of a chore, whatever the situation. You will find suggestions on how to manage the typical ways of using individual whiteboards in your classroom. Follow the guidelines below and the individual whiteboards will be an asset in your lessons.

TYPES OF ACTIVITIES

All successful ways of using resources in the classroom are to some degree planned and targeted. When you plan the use of individual whiteboards for your lesson, your first task is to understand their intended purpose. What do you want to achieve by using them? Is it the best tool at your disposal? Suppose you have decided to use the whiteboards. Then, when you plan your lesson, be clear at what point of the lesson the children will need to use them and how they will do it.

There are three main kinds of activities during which the individual whiteboards can be the right tools to support learning.

PRACTICE

The interplay of teaching and learning governing the structure of any lesson is bound to produce difficulties: sometimes a teacher tends to talk at length leaving little or no opportunities for children to practise. At other times, during most of the lesson children work in silence and, often unknown to the teacher, repeatedly make the same mistakes.

The use of individual whiteboards can be a solution at hand for you and the pupils in these situations. Use them during the whole class teaching to allow children to practise what you are modelling on the board. For example, you may lead a shared writing part of the lesson and model a sentence on the board. Having modelled it, ask the children to write their own sentences on the whiteboards. Allow an opportunity for questions or share some good examples and then move on to the next part.

In Maths, some topics require children to write in order for you to assess how well they understand the concepts you are teaching. One such example can be adding two numbers using partitioning. This problem requires children to perform a few steps and you can establish well the degree to which they understand it when they present it in writing. Another advantage of the whiteboards is that you can practise complex skills or procedures one step at the time. In the example with adding two numbers, you can practise partitioning first and then move on to adding tens and followed by adding the units. Demonstrate how to record each step and allow time for the children to follow your example on their whiteboards. When you feel they are ready for independent work in their books, let them get on with that task. It may be that some children are ready to work independently while others need to practise a bit more. In this case, send those who are ready to the desks and continue to work with the rest on the carpet. Send off individual children to the desks gradually as they become ready to do the tasks independently.

Observing children's calculations or sentence writing on the whiteboards can provide you with the detailed feedback where the children are successful and where they may have some misconceptions. Following up on that feedback, you can decide whether to have an additional whole class session to clarify those misconceptions, an extra small group work or offer individual feedback and corrective actions. The advantage of this approach of assessing the children is that you can adjust your teaching and the flow of the lesson in real time without having to wait until the end of the day to see the work in children's books. Sometimes waiting to see outcomes of children's during the marking at the end of the day is quite late. Many children will have worked for an extensive period of time securing the skills or methods that are wrong. They will be confused the following day having learned and practised something that is incorrect. You will need less time if you can notice the problems early and correct them. Children will spend the lesson time practising and internalising the new knowledge that is accurate.

Practising handwriting and fine motor skills are activities where the whiteboards can be also of great educational value. When purchasing the whiteboards, make sure that they have guide lines on one side. This side can be used by your children to learn to form letters. The use of whiteboards and whiteboard pens for this purpose is especially beneficial for children in early years when their pencil grip is developing and they can still be using a fist or a four-finger grip.

ASSESSMENT

All learning activities need opportunities for assessment. Its purpose is to inform the teacher what pupils know or can do, just as the learning objective tells what the teacher's intention is for pupils' learning outcomes by the end of the lesson. As far as assessment goes, children's ability to do something independently and to explain how they do it are good indicators that they are secure in their learning. How do you quickly assess your pupils' learning as you teach the whole class? Here is where the individual whiteboards can help.

When you teach a particular concept, say adding two two-digit numbers by partitioning them, start with partitioning. Think: are all children able to securely partition the number before moving on to addition? And then try to assess them.

Here are some tips on how you can do it:

- Model how to record partitioning of a two-digit number on the class board.

- Write a different number you want children to partition using the modelled approach.

- Ask the children to hold their whiteboards against their chests and turn them towards you when they have completed. Avoid having the class lifting their boards up.

- If the pupils struggle to keep their answers to themselves try a *1, 2, 3 - show me approach*. It will give time for some to prepare to turn the board towards you but can also be used as a cue for those who show too early.

- Think of quick ways to differentiate to avoid the problems of lagging or rushing – *Now write 'sl' on your boards. Blue table, write two words beginning with 'sl', please.*

- Model individually to those children who need additional help.

- With younger children, to ensure total focus, you may need to teach the *Empty Hands on Your Lap* rule for times when the whiteboards and pens do not need to be used.

Assessing your class *'there and then'* often gives you valuable information - say, the children which still have some misconceptions, or those who do not seem to understand at all. This way is much quicker, more efficient and effective than can be achieved by marking after school or through formal testing. You can even have your own whiteboard on your lap and jot down a list of pupils you wish to talk to further in a small group, allowing others to promptly start independent work.

Another key piece of advice for anybody using the individual whiteboards to assess can be given in five words: 'Only use them when necessary.'

DRAFTING

Teaching mathematical concepts usually requires progression through the following sequence:

- concrete - manipulating physical objects

- representational - dealing with pictorial representations of real objects

- abstract

It is at the representational stage, when children need appropriate tools to help them capture the problem, that whiteboards can be of help both on the carpet and at the desks. Teach children how to solve problems by drawing pictures and use the whiteboards for that.

When writing, young children may find it difficult to perform such a complex task directly in their books - they need to think first, then plan, draft and edit their draft sentences. Ask your pupils to use individual whiteboards to complete these preliminary tasks. The completed sentences then can be copied into the books.

Producing good quality writing with young children who are only beginning to write is never an easy task – far from it. However, going through it methodically, as outlined above, should support you and your children in achieving this goal.

DISTRIBUTING WHITEBOARDS

Store a whiteboard, a pen and a wipe as sets in individual plastic zip folders – one for each pupil. Divide them into two boxes to speed up this process and have two helpers to hand out the folders to the class. This process can be arrange in this way: the class helpers place a number(equal to the number of children in a row) of zip folders on the carpet next to the last child in each row. The children then pass them on along their rows, one folder at a time.

At any rate, keep your children engaged in meaningful activities until everybody has the whiteboard and the pen out. One way to do it is to display a task on the class board so that those who have their whiteboards ready can start working without any delay.

Your helpers should collect the whiteboards the same way as they hand them out – children pass on the boards towards the end of the row. The last child in a row places them on a pile which is then collected by one of the class helpers.

HANDLING RESOURCES

What resources do you keep on the desks all the time and what resources do you store elsewhere and only bring them to the desks when needed? The choice between these two options should be a simple one. The basic rule should be to keep as little as possible permanently on the desks. This way you do not clutter the desk space giving children enough surface to work on and the cleaners to keep the desks clean; you will also reduce unnecessary distractions and the tidying time and effort for the children.

In many of your lessons you have to use many resources. For example, in writing children often need dictionaries, thesauruses, writing prompts and scaffolds. In other subjects, the options may include regular use of equipment, arts supplies and a variety of manipulatives. So, it is inevitable that most of your resources are stored somewhere in the classroom or in the central areas such as Science or Arts cupboards across the school.

Then, how do you effectively manage the use of resources during your lessons? In the first place, plan everything ahead – either during your planning and preparation time or at least the day before you need the resources. Do avoid the issue of leaving it to the day of the lesson. Much stress and many lessons that fall apart can be avoided by good and timely preparations.

EXTERNALLY HELD RESOURCES

Bring any externally held resources to the classroom at least one day before the lesson. It is not surprising that many an experienced and organised teacher discovered some resources missing the day before their lessons. In some cases, when the resources for your lesson are crucial, it is worth checking at least a week in advance making sure that everything is in place. In this case, if anything is missing, you will have plenty of time to locate or order the missing items. One such example worth checking is the batteries. You may want to check that they work in any equipment you are planning to use. Another example that may ruin a well-planned lesson is the laptops that have not been charged. You can prevent an avoidable disappointment by making sure that they have been left to charge overnight.

If you have an additional adult in your classroom such as a teaching assistant, consider assigning the responsibility of bringing the necessary resources to that member of staff. When you plan the lesson, list the resources you need. The day before the lesson your teaching assistant can select the necessary resources, check that everything works and place them in trays on the side in your classroom.

The following day, during the lesson when these resources are going to be used, your classroom helpers can bring the trays to the desks. Ask the helpers to do it only when the children are ready to use the resources, usually during or after your demonstration. If appropriate, remember to go through the steps on how to use the resources safely or not waste them.

At the end of the lesson, or whenever the resources are no longer needed, ask all children to put the resources back in the trays and leave them on their desks. Helpers can then collect the trays and place them on the side somewhere safe in the classroom. Your teaching assistant, or you if you do not have one, can take the resources back during the break time or at the end of the day.

A word about the reading books: at the start of any new school appointment, check how the public library borrowing works. In some areas, book and resource requests need to be made within the first few days of a term in order to arrive at all. In some areas, you may be entitled to a teacher's library card.

RESOURCES HELD IN THE CLASSROOM

Books are one of those resources you have plenty of and need to bring to the desks for every lesson. Keep them in deep trays away from the desks – a single deep tray storage unit is a good solution for that. Helpers can give them out during at the start of the break time. Ask two or three children, or an adult helper, before they go to break to place the books on the desks. The books will be ready for children when they come back to class – children should not wait for the books to be given out at that point. At the end of the lesson, ask children at each desk to place their books on one pile. Ask two or three helpers to collect and place the books into the tray and give out the next set of books.

Internally kept resources should be handled the same

way as the external ones - prepare the resources the day before the lesson and keep them in trays on the side. At the time when you need them at the desks, ask one child from each desk to bring the trays with the resources to the desks. Task the same child with putting the resources back in trays at the end of the session and returning the trays to the places where they collected them from at the start of the lesson.

If you display and share your daily timetable with the class in the morning, state who you want do these activities and what you want to be done. Children will carry out these routines without you having to remind them or explaining what to do at the time when you may have other things to deal with.

Sometimes when you teach very young children, there is a need to use resources on the carpet when children sit in a circle. For that, prepare the necessary resources on the tray and keep it close to the carpet area. After you have settled down the children on the carpet, place the resources in the middle of the circle and ask children to pick one each from the middle. To make this process flow smoothly, decide on the way of choosing the children and avoid the whole class attempting to take the resources from the tray at the same time. You should have no more than one quarter of the class going to the middle at one time to collect the resource. One example is calling one team at a time: Squares, collect one number fan each and move back to your place in the circle.

To hand out the dictionaries and thesauruses, send one child from each desk to bring a set for their desk. At the end of the lesson the class can place the books on a pile in the middle of their desks and the same child can take them back. Later in the year, once the children have settled down and their behaviour is of high standard, train them to collect and return the dictionaries individually and independently whenever they need. Children should not rely on others to bring the dictionaries or thesauruses to the desks.

ASKING AND ANSWERING QUESTIONS

Some people still hold an outdated view of education in schools according to which children are expected do what they are told. To master effective learning skills, children have to be able to contribute to the lessons and actively participate in them. Children need to be taught to ask questions and articulate their answers with precision. They will also need to use a relevant and broad vocabulary bank, good reasoning skills and ability to express their thoughts and feelings verbally.

TEACHER ASKING QUESTIONS

Knowing what you want to establish can help you decide on the way you ask your questions. When deciding on the approach to questioning for assessment purposes, you may want to find out the following:

- group learning - what children from different groups, such as attainment, disadvantaged or gender groups - have learned

- individual learning – how well certain pupils are progressing

- class learning - overall assessment of learning in your class

Bear in mind that questioning is used not only for assessment. It is a complex communication tool which can improve your understanding of children's needs, engage and motivate them.

Here are some general rules that apply to all ages.

Conciseness

Keep your questions short. Few children can memorise all information in a long-winded question. So, your question has to give only crucial information. If you really need to say more, ask a few separate questions. In questioning, conciseness and precision make for effectiveness.

Differentiation

Questions, apart from being a tool of formative assessment, help pupils make connections with prior knowledge and stimulate cognitive development. Ask the questions at the right level of challenge for each child and rephrase or simplify your questions if necessary.

Visual cues

Visual cues enable you to communicate the information more quickly and help you reinforce the message. With visual reinforcement, children absorb the information more readily. Visual cues also have other advantage - they help to keep your pupils' attention. Here are some ideas that will help you:

- hold up or point to objects or pictures to help your pupils visualise the problem;

- point at the technical words you are using – prepare and display them in advance;

- use gestures to help convey the meaning.

Children's interests

Keep your questions interesting. If you know your children well, put your questions in the context of their interests. For instance, if a child is interested in football it could be something like this: *Charlie, a football team requires two bottles of water per player plus one for a coach. How many bottles should be ordered?*

Targeted questions

This is where you decide who you want to ask. What do you want your question to reveal? How do you adapt your question to the child?

Asking a targeted question should not be difficult if you know exactly what you want to find out. Start with a name of the child. It will draw his or her attention. You want to be sure that when you ask the question, the child is listening. Allow time for the child to focus. Here are some examples of different targeted questions.

Michael, how much is two plus three?

Leyla, explain the difference between experiment hypothesis and conclusion?

Jude, look at these shapes. Touch the shape that has three sides. Followed by What is the name of this shape?

When you ask a targeted question, you know the child you are asking. So, adapt your question accordingly. A child who is new to English is unlikely to answer a question full of difficult or technical words. Similarly, a shy child who is unwilling to speak in front of the class may not say the names of the correct shapes but can still point at them.

Random selection

Just pick up a name in random, and ask that pupil a question. When determining on how to select a pupil randomly, decide on what may work best for you. For example, prepare at the beginning of the year a class set of lolly sticks with names of your children. Have the children's names written at the bottom parts of the sticks. Then, each time you want to select a child at random, pick a tub of lolly sticks and pull out one of the sticks.

The routine may look something like this: *I am going now to pull out a lolly stick with a name of a child.* Pick a lolly stick at this point and read out the name. *Stephen, please explain how some foods can be harmful for your body.*

Allow and expect children to take time to think before they give an answer. In a primary school, approximately four to seven seconds of thinking time is a good guide of what that time might be.

Searching questions

Good questions should:

- be purposeful

- arouse interest

- be open

- encourage thinking

It is obviously easier to achieve these objectives when asking a particular child. Asking the whole class, however, is more challenging as you usually face a broad range of abilities and interests. Searching questions are typically formed in such a way that they can be understood and answered by all children. Here are some examples:

What do you know about Ancient Egypt?

Name three devices in your homes that use electricity.

Why should we go on a trip to the forest?

It may be difficult to remember the key questions for assessment in the midst of other pressures, particularly in a new environment. Consider jotting them down on paper notes or have a set of questions or lesson prompts which can be displayed on the interactive board for the whole class. The latter approach is especially useful for older children when the questions become more complex and may require supplementary graphics. By displaying the questions on the board, you will allow children to access them independently.

CHILDREN ANSWERING QUESTIONS

Traditionally, a teacher expects children to put their hands up when they want to answer a question. This way of answering helps the teacher choose a child wishing to offer an answer. While this routine of asking questions has its merits and place, it can also limit the teacher's ability to use questioning as an effective tool.

Decide how you want your pupils to let you know that they have an answer. Think about the personalities of your pupils. In every class, there are children who are confident or want attention. They like putting their hands up. On the other hand, there are those who may want to answer but find the prospect of talking in front of everyone quite daunting. Yet, other children need a bit of encouragement. Once chosen, they are often willing to talk at length. You will need a routine which would encourage all pupils to put themselves forward with an answer.

Here is one way how you can do it.

Teach your pupils to put their thumbs up when they have an answer. They can do it by showing their thumbs up against their chests when ready. In this way, you can help those who are a little shy not to be intimidated by the raised hands. Another benefit of this approach is avoiding putting pressure on children to rush with an answer. They will spend time thinking rather than being distracted by the other pupils' hands.

Children tend to answer the questions in simple ways. Often, their answers are presented in a form of one word or a phrase. To receive a quality answer from a child who has something to offer, two ingredients are needed: the questions must be well formulated and the child has to be taught how to answer well. Both of the ingredients require the teacher's input.

Model how to answer your questions. Make it clear what you want to find out and what information can help you. One of the ways children learn is by imitating others. When teaching them to answer questions, ensure it is you they imitate - not their peers who may not necessarily do it well themselves. Following these key rules will help:

- Model how to structure the answers;

- Model how to answer using full sentences;

- Draw children's attention to the use of technical or precise vocabulary in their answers;

- Teach them how to back up opinions or choices with

reasons;

- Teach children how to evaluate and improve their answers.

Give an opportunity to speak to every child. Before you ask any child to give you an answer, ask the class to give their answers to a partner next to them. In this case, every child will have a chance to offer an answer in a non-intimidating way. Then, ask one or two children to share with the rest what their partner told them. Remember that some children tend to take over the conversation and will talk all time not allowing their partner to have a turn. Control this process by giving one minute for one partner to talk then direct the children to swap so that the one who talked will listen and vice versa. Anticipate and manage the difficulty when confident children simply wait for a turn to speak and the answers already given by others are being repeated. Teach your class to expand on the answers of their peers: *Tasneem says we need to multiply the number. Who can suggest a useful method for it?* At the beginning, when teaching children not to repeat the initial answer, say: *Tasneem made an excellent suggestion. Can anyone tell us why it is a good idea?*

PUPILS ASKING QUESTIONS

Any lesson is a two-way process. The teacher and the children are both the participants and the owners of it. Learning, being a journey, requires stopping points for the teacher and the pupils to recalibrate their bearings and to make sure they are on the right track.

Suppose you are teaching a new concept. You cannot expect much in the way of understanding and will look for children's focus and their attempts to connect the new learning to what they already know. You will therefore plan to concentrate in your lesson on teaching one small part of the concept at a time, and you should make the most of engaging the children. Structure your teaching in a way that allows short portions of new learning to be followed by opportunities for children to check that they understand you correctly. For that, pause regularly to see whether the children have any questions or want you to clarify something. Ask them to explain their understanding of what you have just explained. Be certain that they can explain or, at least can illustrate using suitable examples, their understanding before you proceed any further.

Tell your pupils beforehand that you will be stopping from time to time giving them opportunities to ask questions. Knowing it in advance will make them worry less when they are not sure whether they follow you correctly during the teaching part of the lesson. It also means that you are less likely to have children sitting with raised hands rather than listening to you while you are teaching.

Of course, if children are confident asking you questions, let them speak. But watch out for those who are timid and need encouragement to ask a question. Some children, especially those having an adult supporting them, may find it easier to engage with the adult rather than the class. Train your support staff and involve them by making sure that you have feedback from those children as well.

Whether or not your pupils ask questions or seek clarification, use formative assessment at these points to be sure that all children understand what you have just taught. Use that information to adjust the current lesson or to plan the future one.

TRANSITIONS BETWEEN ACTIVITIES

What you are aiming for in any successful transition you want to implement can be summed up in three words – structure, clarity, and speed. They are, in fact, the ABC of all effective transitions. The best thing you can do for your pupils in this respect is to give them a sense of stability and order.

The transitions between activities within lessons – new session, interventions, tuition, streaming – are essentially the structured actions designed to end one activity and begin the next one in the most efficient way.

The components of the transition are straightforward enough:

1. Completion of the preceding activity

2. Preparation of the workplace and resources for the next activity

3. Start of the next activity.

None of this poses any particular difficulties: the structure and implementation of your routines often share common features and are determined by the particular activities your children are involved in.

It is your responsibility as a teacher to direct the course of your day. To ensure smooth progress from one activity to another, you should plan your day and make the necessary arrangements for it beforehand. It pays to prepare the resources in advance and instruct any additional adults about the structure of the day and their roles.

WHOLE CLASS TRANSITION

Hardly any single unit of teaching starts and finishes with break times. A typical lesson is composed of many interlinked parts. And the more parts there are, the more transitions there are in the lesson. Skilful steering of your class through the lesson among other things requires clarity and consistency of your routines. With this approach, you will guarantee smooth transition from one part of your lesson to another maintaining children's focus and classroom order. The best thing you can do for your children in this respect is to make the most of your session in the given time.

Closing the preceding session

This requires a structured approach – not just to what you do but to the actions of your class. Before you sum up the lesson, make sure that you are ready and have enough time to do it. First, get the attention of your class using one of the routines you have already established in your class. Speak when children have turned towards you and are paying attention to what you are about to say. At this point sum up what has been learned in the lesson, praise and reward individuals or groups for the work. If relevant, suggest any ideas on how children can expand on this at home.

The next step is to ensure that children clear all unnecessary resources from the desks and put away the books. For this, follow your usual routine by instructing your classroom helpers to put away the resources and books while others tidy up their desks. Once the children have finished, they should sit at their desks ready for the next part. Keep an eye on the time they take to complete this task by displaying a countdown timer on the board. You should expect children to tidy their desks and settle down within one minute. As children tidy their desks, walk around the classroom and point out good examples where the desks have been cleared properly and the children worked well as a team. Reward good work using the established reward system in your class. At the same time, draw children's attention where your expectations of tidying and team work are not being met by telling or showing them how to improve.

Preparing for the next activity

Now that the children have completed tidying their desks and are sitting ready for the next part, get their full attention again. Tell your class what the next lesson is going to be and what they need to do before the start.

At this point you may need to bring a new set of resources. Also, your groupings may change for that lesson and the children should move to different desks. As in the previous part, instruct the children what you want them to do and tell them how much time they have for that. Unless you have lengthy arrangements to perform, such as for ICT or Arts, this part should also take no longer than one minute. Use the timer to help children stay focused on the tasks.

Starting the next session

With the whole class paying full attention, start the next session. To start on a positive note, remind your class how capable they are of working hard, listening and producing work of the high standard. This will pay off throughout the lesson. Children who want your praise with strive to meet your expectations and will see you noticing and recognising their effort. Now, when all children are ready, introduce the new lesson.

GROUP TRANSITION

It is hard to imagine a primary school class where children always stay with their class teacher. In practice, every day you have individual children or groups working in your classroom or outside with different adults. These arrangements are planned either by you or others and can include interventions, therapy, music tuition or streaming such as phonics or catch up sessions. All these provisions try to balance two conflicting elements – the interruption to the learning led by the teacher in the classroom, and the necessity to meet the children's needs. It can become disruptive as children need to stop the class work, often leave and then return to the classroom later. Having returned and missed out a portion of the lesson, the children need to be reintegrated into the class work. It often requires the teacher to attend to these children as they do not know what to do. The disruption caused by all of the mentioned above inconveniences can be reduced if you have clear routines to handle them. So too with children independently following the routines: if they have everything prepared for that session rather than rely on you.

Some routines may not lend themselves to being carried out by children independently. For example, you may not expect them upon the return to the classroom to start the work which the rest of the children are doing. Two possible reasons for that may be that there is not enough time or the children who return to the classroom have missed the main part of the lesson when you were teaching. One way of dealing with it is to allocate time to work with those children by going through the learning that they have missed while away from the classroom. If there is not enough time left in the lesson or you are engaged with others, have a set of prepared tasks which children can collect and do independently or with little initial guidance.

For Maths and English, have a few trays of work or wallets on the wall for children who have missed all but a small part of the lesson. Have work that children need to consolidate on laminated cards. In Maths, it can be challenges or problem cards. In English, the choice of grammar, spelling and sentence work can offer children an opportunity to work independently on the topics covered in class. The laminated cards can be filled in with whiteboard pens and then cleaned when finished. Ready-made short reading comprehension sheets is another excellent option for children when timings do not go to plan.

Leaving the classroom

How do you organise a pupil or a group of children to leave your classroom with minimum disruption to you and to the remaining children? One effective approach is this: have all the resources necessary for that activity prepared and placed in an easy to access area. And, if possible, train the children to prepare the resources in advance. This could be as simple as placing a reading book near the door at the start of the lesson during which the child will be stepping out for an additional reading comprehension session. You should rehearse with them, if you can, to expect a signal from you by which they will know what to do. But if these occasions are rare, or if each time it is different children who go out, by all means guide them there and then what you want them to do. Simply call out the child's name and instruct him or her what to do. For example: *Safya, close your book and put it in the middle of the desk. Take your pencil and a ruler and go with Ms Smith.*

When a group of children is sent to another place during the lesson, they are usually collected by another adult or go there by themselves. In the case that an adult comes to collect the children, they should line up outside the classroom with that adult being in charge. If you have to send a group on their own, line them up inside the classroom and send them off when everyone is ready. In this way you can supervise the group.

It often happens that when children attend additional activities, they do not go empty-handed – books, pencils, rulers, musical instruments are but a few examples of what they may need to take with them. If you know what resources the children need for the session, get them ready in advance. Place the items in an easy to access place so that when the groups need to leave, all they have to do is to line up, collect the resources and leave the classroom quietly. Older children can be expected to make these preparations independently. You want to avoid children wandering around the classroom, disrupting others or asking you where the books or pencils are. As regards musical instruments, have these brought to school on the day of the tuition and stored somewhere safe away from areas which are frequently used. Children will collect the instruments when they go to their lessons and place them back when they return. Pencils and rulers are usually in use at the desks so children will have to collect these as they leave their desks. Books can be prepared in advance and placed in easy to access areas. One child can collect the books when the group leave the classroom and put them back in the same place when the children return to class.

When children leave the classroom alone, expect a young child to be collected by an adult. Older and more responsible children can safely travel alone short distances around the school. Check that they know where they are going. But remember to train your pupils to return to your classroom immediately if the adult they expect to work with is not there.

Returning to the classroom

When children return from the activity, either individually or as a group, expect them to enter the classroom and then knock on the door. They should wait for your acknowledgement and directions. Check that everyone is back and enquire about anyone unaccounted for. Signal to the children what to do next – it can be a gesture or a verbal direction. For example, you can use your hand to point towards the carpet area. Alternatively, say: *The group at the door, come and sit down on the carpet.*

If your class are engrossed in activities and the working atmosphere in the classroom is such that you may not hear children knocking on the door, the group should wait while one of the children approaches you to let you know that they are back.

If you expect the returned children to do different work to what the rest of the class do, have it ready on your desk. Upon their return, sit the group on the carpet and go through the work with them before sending the children to their desks.

If your classroom space allows for it, have an additional desk. Not to distract other children working at their desks, use this desk to go over the work with a child who has missed part of the lesson. Another good use of this desk is for one-to-one work with children.

INDIVIDUAL TRANSITION

However well you prepare your lesson, you are bound to find yourself facing situations when pupils complete their work early in the lesson – some may take you by surprise, and some may be the pupils who regularly go through their work at speed. Whatever the case, be prepared to keep those children continuously engaged in learning.

Be clear nonetheless that your pupils know what you mean by completing their work. It is worth pointing out to them the difference between a task and learning. The tasks are selected to help pupils to learn particular skills or to deepen their understanding of something. There may be situations that children successfully complete the tasks simply by following the techniques modelled by the teacher although they do not understand what they are doing. Yet at other times, children may understand the concepts well but are confused by the task or cannot access it simply due to the language barrier. To avoid such scenarios, use your formative assessment procedures to be certain that pupils possess deep understanding as well as are able to use the techniques of the new learning you are trying to instil. When that is the case, move them on.

It is worth teaching your children to identify the situations when they may not have completed the tasks but seem to understand clearly what it is all about – they may be ready for the next step. While older pupils may recognise these situations independently, the younger ones need to rely on you – the class teacher - to spot them during the lesson and guide the children to the next step as necessary. Ultimately, it is your judgement whether the children need to move on or continue to practise.

Forward planning and preparation are crucial here. Avoid having children who follow you or put their hands up to tell you that they have finished their work. Sometimes, when children think that they finished their task, they start to misbehave. Others, and this is harder to notice, sit quietly wasting time and waiting until the break time starts. Incorporate your success criteria discussions into the beginning of your lessons. Children need to be clear from the start what successful completion of learning should look like. Decide on the format of your success criteria; it can be a modelled sample displayed at the front on a large sheet of paper; or a check list of the requirements to be met; or a descriptive outline of what you expect. Teach your children how to use the success criteria to judge the degree of completion of their work. And if the criteria have been met, teach the children how they can choose what to do next.

In its simplest form the next step may be for the children to attempt to do the work of the next up ability group. Be cautious though - it may not always be appropriate or yield the best possible outcomes for those children.

The purpose of the independent work is to deepen children's understanding of the concepts, make meaningful links between different concepts and sharpen their technical skills. And there are different ways which can help to achieve it.

Extension work

As mentioned earlier, this can simply take the form of a child attempting to do the work of the next up ability group. During the planning stage, consider this option if the work is closely related. If the resources are needed for this task, prepare a few additional sets to give to the children who will move on to do this work. This approach should be considered when you are not required to teach a child anything new – the child should be able to access the work independently.

Investigative work can be considered as the means of deepening children's understanding of the taught concepts. Again, the children should not rely on you to provide one-to-one support in this case but be able to proceed unaided. Here are a few examples from different subjects.

- When working with coins in year 1, a child can be asked to investigate all possible combinations of up to four coins that make 10p.

- In early years, a child can be asked to explore how many different colours he or she can make by mixing two colours from a given a set of three colours.

- When writing a story in upper KS2, a child can be asked to explore an impact on suspense of a variety of possible ways to open the story - a description of the scene, a character's monologue or a depiction of an action.

You can follow up these activities with some questions. It will allow you to assess children's understanding, their use of language and ability to draw conclusions based on observations.

Supporting others

Good learning in a class setting rarely happens in isolation. Team work and collaboration skills are a cornerstone to success both at school and then later in employment or entrepreneurship. Create opportunities for children to work with partners or in teams and you can help them learn the practical skills of successful collaboration. They will also learn how to manage the inevitable minor conflicts that arise from learning in close quarters.

Children enjoy helping others, the confidence they gain is transferable also to new learning opportunities and their own understanding is deepened through verbalisation of the skills they are trying to reach others. Many children will surprise you by being able to complete a process, while still needing regular practice to gain the necessary vocabulary and verbal skills to communicate to others how they do it. If you have a child who has completed his or her work, utilise this teaching capacity in your class. They can support those at their desks who may find the work a bit challenging and can benefit from peers helping them produce better quality work. Or, they can work with children at other desks.

Children who receive support will be able to have someone to go through the work with them on a one-to-one basis.

These children will have a chance to ask questions or observe something modelled to them. The children who are helping can share their own work thus showing the standards to be aimed for and providing a more accessible model for those who are visual learners.

Equally, there is a great benefit to those who are helping. By explaining the concepts to another child, they deepen their own understanding of the taught ideas. Such collaboration is especially powerful when these children use relevant technical vocabulary, objects or pictorial representations to demonstrate the principles and share examples from life.

Be cautious though not to rely on this support to replace your input for children who need additional support. Your helpers cannot be expected to do the work of an experienced teacher. With good training, modelling and balanced approach, there is still place for this kind of collaboration to benefit all your children.

Personalised learning

Successful learning experiences are often child-led. When the child completes his or her work and is ready to move on, personalisation can be an answer for success in many cases. Considering children's interests and needs can be a powerful motivational tool for them.

You often set personalised targets for individual children. These targets reflect their current needs or gaps in learning. Planning a regular dedicated time for a child to work on his or her personalised targets can be a challenge. So, whenever individual children complete their work early in the lesson, and their outcomes meet your expectations, consider directing these children to work on their targets. With time and age, you should expect them to be able to do it without having to be reminded about it. In early years though, children still depend heavily on the adults in class to suggest possible ideas or be directed towards suitable activities. So, any personalisation for the youngest pupils will require an adult to set up a suitable activity and assist the children.

Another possible alternative you have is allowing children to use technology to practise certain skills – spellings, phonics, times tables – or carry out independent research. The research may be linked to the class curriculum topics or be of personal interest to that child. Whatever they do, children must be always clear of the personal learning outcomes they are pursuing.

With the use of ICT, care should be taken not to have children form an opinion that tablets or laptops is something to aim for. They may start producing sub-standard work rushing to get some time on the devices. Also, you should consider the impact on the children who hardly ever have an opportunity to complete their work and use the technology for some research or project work. You can easily account for the latter during the lesson planning stage when you decide on the tasks for the independent work. Select the tasks that these children can reasonably be expected to complete in short time. It can offer them a chance to engage in other learning activities with the help of technology at hand.

Fostering the love for learning in children often requires you to be the driving force behind it. Wise stewardship of educational opportunities on your part can make this very likely to happen. Incorporate children's views and interests into your lessons. It will give them the sense of ownership and pride. But it takes time - and sometimes a truly remarkable results can only be seen after a few years of consistent and dedicated work with children.

PEER AND SELF-ASSESSMENT

Achieving the highest quality of work is as important in the classroom as completing it. It is not enough when children do what they are told: they must be active learners. Attention, enthusiasm, courage, motivation, curiosity, tenacity and hard work – all should combine to tell the teacher that the children are doing their utmost to gain from the lesson.

Create an environment in which these qualities are valued and celebrated. Introduce significant rewards, such as Star of the Week or send personal postcards home. Combine it with whichever rewards your school uses and praise publicly children of all abilities who show initiative in learning and strive to achieve well in school.

It is to their skills as independent learners that children will owe their success. Being an independent learner is one of the best ways of achieving success in school, as well as later in private and business life. As with so many other things, success in learning depends on a person's ability to reflect and critically evaluate own work. Children should also be capable of giving constructive feedback to others.

Peer and self-assessment can take two forms – assessment against the criteria check list and evaluative assessment. Assessment against the check list is suitable for children from early years. Evaluative assessment on the other hand, is more complex requiring critical thinking skills in evaluating the quality of work and ability to verbally convey it to others. Such assessment is more suitable for older children - starting from the age of seven or eight would be a sensible approach for you to introduce it.

SELF-ASSESSMENT VS SELF-MARKING

Self-assessment is not quite the same thing as self-marking. The difference is one of impact on the child vs impact on the work – learning vs level.

Self-marking, however desirable it may be for the workload reduction purposes, often bears little or no benefit for both the teacher and the child. A piece of writing or completed task can hardly hope to be acceptably self-marked for two main reasons – poor accuracy and reliability.

Poor accuracy of self-marking is closely related to pupil ability. Self-marking against the success criteria skews the results upwards as pupils tend to overstate the marks. Most able pupils can, at best, produce moderate quality of self-marking.

Bias is evident in both peer and self-marking. Friendship groups, cultural and deprivation backgrounds are a few factors that distort marking reliability. Gender bias also plays a significant role – boys tend to be more confident in their own performance.

Paradoxically then, it takes more time and effort for the teacher. Having little confidence in the accuracy of the self-marked results, the teacher feels forced to check through the work anyway. The process can become needlessly cumbersome and time consuming. And especially so when children are expected to set their own goals, leave feedback for the teacher and record all that in their books.

But what is always possible is self-assessment – reflection and growth. That is conscious self-monitoring and improvement actions taken by the children at every step of their learning.

Even the best and most efficient teachers find it impossible to go through each step of child's learning in fine details: identify developmental needs, suggest corrective actions and watch over the immediate improvements made by the child. Even if it was possible, such activities would hardly be of benefit to the child in the long term – reliance on the teacher to 'spoon-feed' leads to apathy and over-dependence on adults. Helping children to be reflective, attentive to details, seek improvement and value own growth is the answer. Form the environment where children take responsibility for their achievements, where they want to improve and have the skills how to do it. Create the learning culture that is owned and nurtured by them.

So, an unmarked piece of work reflected upon and improved by a child can still have a significant educational impact. At the same time, an extensively marked, commented on and levelled piece of work by the teacher may not be adding anything to the progress of the pupil.

SELF-ASSESSMENT

When used well, self-assessment can be a valuable learning tool in your classroom. So, like with all other routines, teach your children how to do it well.

First, children need to be able to self-assess independently. They should know what to look for and, when found, what to do with it. This process can be described in three words – inspect, identify, improve.

Secondly, they need to know when to do it. Your goal should be to establish the ways of working which would help your children to continuously assess and improve their work. What's more, it has to be unprompted by you. They can achieve it if they do this regularly.

Teaching children to self-assess

Initially, you will need to teach your children how to do it. You can structure your training process in the following way.

- Explain to the children the benefits of self-assessment– sell it to them. It is important that they know why they are doing it and, that they value the idea. Embed the culture of learning in which there is no fear of making errors - quite the opposite. Children should want to find every way they can be better and share it with others when they have done so. Be sure to notice and celebrate it.

- Select a suitable example of work, display it on the board and model how to assess it against your success criteria. For the training purposes, select no more than two success criteria to assess against.

- Model how to scan the work and to identify the examples where the criteria have been met. Suppose you are modelling this using a piece of writing and your success criterion is the use of adverbs to clarify the actions. For that, read through the text and underline the verbs.

- Follow it up by looking at each underlined verb. Now, underline the adverbs used in the text.

- Next, look at the verbs again. Identify which ones have no adverbs and may need clarity. For instance, the text has a phrase scurrying along the unlit alley and children feel that there is scope for improvement. Show how to reflect on why this part needs to be clarified. Is the phrase too vague? Or, does the sentence not have the desired impact on the reader?

Whatever the reason, children need to know why they are doing it. Never encourage the 'up-levelling' culture when children are taught to stuff their writing with everything they can think of making them believe that the more they add, the higher the level.

- Ask the children to suggest possible adverbs that could improve the clarity of the verb. Discuss the suggested alternatives and decide on the best adverbs to use. Make sure that all children understand the meaning of the words. At this point, encourage and show how to use a thesaurus to select the best possible word.

- Insert the adverb into the text. If space does not allow for this, show children how to use indices. One simple way to do it is to indicate with a letter or a number the place where the insertion needs to be made. Then, in the margin or at the bottom of the page, write that number or letter - whichever you use – followed by a word or a phrase for the insertion.

Now, allow children to practise the modelled skills. Display another short piece of writing and ask them to perform the same activity using the new text. You can challenge some by giving them a different success criterion when they complete this task. To help children navigate through their marking, show how to use different lines – straight, double, curved, dotted or dashed lines – to distinguish between different aspects they are trying to highlight. For example, all verbs can be highlighted with straight lines while adverbs can be indicated with curved lines. This will help them to locate quickly the necessary parts of sentences.

As children practise, observe them and offer personalised feedback. For major misconceptions, stop the class and explain again before the children go any further making mistakes. Consider carrying out the part of training where children learn to self-assess independently one step at a time. Move on to the next part of the training only when the children are secure. Review and give feedback after each step. It is important that all children learn how to do it well at this stage. Having a few modelling and training sessions may be necessary for younger children; some of your children may need on-going support for some time.

Guidance

Having explained and trained the children how to self-assess and improve own work, you cannot expect them to remember such a complex procedure. To make it work and be part of their daily routines, it needs to be summarised and displayed as guidance in prominent, easy to see places in your classroom. Initially, you may need this guidance to be very detailed to make sure that children do not end up interpreting short statements in the wrong way. With time, and to free up the classroom display space, you can simplify the guidance and display it in the form of clear steps. Keep full the guidance for those who may need it for longer or for the children who join your class mid-term. Decide where you want to display the guidance. The choice of walls, books or desks is there for you to select from.

If you go for walls, make sure that there are a few identical displays spread across your classroom so that children from every desk can see it clearly. You can also consider having laminated guidance cards on the desks. As in the case with wall displays, make sure that wherever the children sit, the guidance has to be easily accessible for them to see and use.

Consistency

More important than the training and the guidance is the need to be consistent. Having trained children and displayed the self-assessment guidance for them, make sure that they do it – at every opportunity. The air of stability in your classroom, so important for winning the children round, tends to disperse increasingly with each inconsistency that they notice. Hence the need to remind the children - and yourself - to follow the routines habitually. And remember to refer them to the guidance which they should use independently without the need for you to go over the steps each time.

Initially, you may find it more effective if you plan the dedicated time for self-assessment. During your lessons, constantly remind the children to assess their work against the success criteria and improve it. Remember not to leave it to the end of the lesson. If the goal is to train children to use self-assessment and improve on a continuous basis, then it is better for them to learn to do it as they go through the lesson. Later, as children get used to doing it regularly, give personalised feedback to help them hone their skills. Soon you will find them confident and capable at both self-assessment and independent improvement.

Consider this easy yet effective approach for your classroom. Have a long strip with named clothes pegs along it. Whenever a child edits and improves a piece of writing, or presents a good example of self-assessment, photocopy the page and add it to the peg line. Children enjoy seeing a selection of work build up on their pegs. Over time, they can use it to easily view and share their achievements. It also serves as an excellent prompt for those children who wish to improve their own writing and seek ideas on how to do it.

One last point. Always notice and praise success. How else can you promote the use of good habits?

PEER ASSESSMENT

Apart from self-assessment, which is likely to be more frequent, peer assessment is another valuable tool at your disposal. While these two forms of assessment share many common features, there are some distinctive differences between them.

The skill of peer assessment is well worth teaching. For one thing, a second opinion and sound reflection give children the feeling of comfort and security. Knowing that they have had a partner to go through their work with can reduce anxiety about the work being wrong, create opportunities to ask questions and share ideas and examples of work. It is especially compelling as peer assessment can be done frequently which cannot be said about the possibility for you to work with every child. The knowledge gained through collaboration with a partner can be a potent step in motivating your children to gain the most from working together.

When training children to do peer assessment, you may want to leave it until later in the year after you have secured the skills and practice of self-assessment. Of course, if your new class have been well trained in self-assessment by the previous teacher, start the peer assessment early in the year. If they practised both forms of assessment in the previous years, you may want to review whether those practices meet your expectations. Decide what you want to do. Your choice is either to run a quick refresher lesson or, if the previous routines do not meet your requirements, to train the children your routines for peer and self-assessment.

Teaching children to peer assess

By now your children should be familiar with the concept of self-assessment and know its purpose. They should also have experienced the benefits of it which would help you with the introduction of peer assessment. The essential training parts to do are:

- Model how to do the peer assessment using a sample piece of work.

- For most practical purposes keeping the children at their desks and pairing them up with someone next to them will suffice. It avoids the need to move them around the classroom and difficulties associated with pairing children from different ability groups.

- Let children practise in pairs – give feedback and allow time for questions.

- Display and explain the types of comments they can make about their partner's work.

- Practise and use verbal peer-to-peer feedback first. Only when the children are secure, proceed with giving the written feedback. The transition should include the combination of verbal feedback first followed by a short comment which would help the pupil to retrieve the conversation from memory.

- Teach and manage confidentiality in peer assessments – children should not discuss with others their peer-to-peer work or comment on it.

- Allow fair opportunities for each partner to give and receive feedback.

- Offer opportunities to peer assess the same work again once the feedback has been acted upon. This activity will allow the children to reflect on and evaluate two things – how well the feedback was given by one partner and how successfully it was acted upon by another.

Once you have practised peer assessment for some time, children's confidence and their ability to quality assess and give feedback on their peers' work will grow. If initially the process is too complex, especially for the younger children threatening to dishearten or confuse them, use the simple first phase. In this phase, teach your children how to analyse, work together and discuss possible improvements. You will expand the routine later, when they are ready.

TIDYING UP

As with everything, to achieve efficiency you need to be organised. Your children also need to be taught the skills of organisation. The first step to it is to have the right equipment.

Keep a tray and holders for pencils, pens, rulers on each desk. Show the children how to place all equipment neatly into the trays in the middle of the desks. Teach them how to put the pencil shavings in the bin, how not to waste paper and use the recycling bin for scrap paper. The fewer permanently kept items are on the children's desks, the easier it is for them to keep the desks tidy. There will also be enough space for children to work comfortably. Keep the writing prompts, the hundred squares, number fans and other occasionally used resources at a side resource base in your classroom. Teach your children to collect these resources when they need them and return them back at the end of the lesson. Just as with teaching children to use the dictionaries independently, initially you may need a helper to give out and collect these aids.

Have storage areas clearly marked and teach children

how to put away the toys. When training the children to tidy up, demonstrate how to collect and place the items into the correct storage boxes. You can demonstrate it to them by putting away one type of equipment at a time and then giving them an opportunity to practise. Once you have explained and shown what to do, use a few of your most capable children to demonstrate while others watch. Follow on to the next area or equipment and select the next group of children to model after you have explained what to do. These processes do take some time at the start of the year but the benefit in saved time and gained learning you achieve later by far outweighs the time spent to train the children.

When it is tidy up time, select a group of children from the overcrowded areas and direct them to those places that do not have enough children to tidy up so that everyone completes the tidying up at the same time. Bring in some fun and competition into the routine – children will see it as fun activity rather than a chore. Act out different creatures such as robots or elephants tidying up your classroom. Keep an eye on it though not to allow the children to get carried away and play games instead of tidying.

BREAKS

Rest when you're weary. Refresh and renew yourself, your body, your mind, your spirit. Then get back to work.

RALPH MARSTON

School should be a practical place, and children's experiences there should be positive. Studies show that children behave well, focus and learn better in school when they are rested and happy. For example, eight-year-old children can only concentrate for up to 40 minutes before they need to have a break in school. But break does not necessarily mean that they need to go outside after every 40 minutes of learning. A practical and smart planning of the day with active physical movements will be sufficiently adequate in helping children to stretch and refocus making them ready for the next learning session.

SMALL BREAKS

When your lessons are well structured, stimulating and you have high expectations of children's behaviour, you know that they will work hard and learn fast. You would therefore anticipate them to get tired and to need rest throughout the day.

One simple way to accommodate such rests is to plan small breaks between activities. These can take many forms – from an on-the-spot brief physical exercise when children stretch their muscles to a five-minute run around on the playground to get some fresh air. They can be light-hearted, serious, or a mixture of both. Like any other short activity, the various kinds of small breaks have the advantage of flexibility.

For a short, on-the-spot break use physical activities beside the desks. They enable children to stretch their muscles, rest their eyes and regain focus after prolonged times at the desks. A short, full of energy burst of action will prove of great benefit to both the educational aims and the wellbeing of your children. It will allow you to prepare children for the next activity when you want them to pay full attention to what you are going to teach. There is a great choice of commercially available five-minute activities on DVDs that you can purchase. Alternatively, have a selection of your favourite music and lead the activities yourself. Note that not only are these active pauses in the day beneficial to the children – you, the adult, need short breaks too. You need to keep your focus and replenish your energy to give your best in the lesson.

Five minutes outside – preferably a brisk walk together or a short run around the playground – has much the same advantages as the physical activity in class with the added bonus of fresh air, a drink of water and some exposure to sunlight. Make sure you are aware of the PE timetable and the outdoor space bookings. Use the playground when it is empty - walking out into a football game will have the opposite to the desired effect.

Reading a passage from a book, sharing a class story, watching and discussing the latest news or fascinating facts are but a few examples of what else you can do to break a long lesson into smaller, more concentrated parts. Make sure, however, that the short breaks you use are both treats and the devices to maintain high level of participation and learning in your lessons - it is you who should decide when they happen. Or, you can make them conditional – of, say, children's standards of work and quality of their participation in the lesson. A word of warning. Avoid turning to YouTube or other online video streaming websites for treats. Any such channel with adverts or automatic play features is too unpredictable for classroom use and is best saved for home. If you have to use it, play the video beforehand and check that it does not have any unsuitable materials to which you may unwittingly expose your children.

REST TIME IN EARLY YEARS

With lots of stimulation, both physical and mental, it is no surprise that young children tire easily and need to rest. Regular rest time at school sometimes is the only opportunity during the day for them to relax, to make up for the loss of sleep at night and to recover their concentration for learning. The rest time is essential in early years - you need alert and focused children in your lessons. Expect to plan and allocate the total of about 30-45min for it throughout the day.

Have a quiet corner with pillows, soft light and blankets where children can spend some time to rest or to calm down. Set up a quiet den or a pop-up tent to relieve them from visual stimulation. Provide books and model reading alone, or quietly sharing a book with a friend. The rest does not necessarily mean that children need to sleep although this option should also be considered. Not all children know how to calm down and rest. You will need to manage this process and guide some of them as necessary.

In the early years, it is very easy for children to find themselves in a very busy room with laminated prompts and pictures hanging in every imaginable place. Avoid the onslaught of information everywhere. Keep a good balance between stimulating and secure learning environment when preparing a classroom for the new year.

A simple way to manage this is to plan your day carefully. Try to achieve a sensible balance of active and quiet times, of group work with times to work alone. And remember also to set up your room at the start of the year to allow for quiet areas and busy spaces to be separate.

TOILET BREAKS

Teach the toilet routine as soon as possible. Children should go to the toilet when they need it and preferably during break or lunch times.

On the first day of school, take your class around the building and show them where the toilets are located. Show them which toilet they have to use when they leave the classroom during the lesson and, if different, which toilet during the breaks. Do not assume that they remember it from the previous year – the toilets for different year groups may be different and you may have new children in your class. Show them the route they need to take when going to the toilet from the classroom.

When teaching young children, show where the toilet paper is, how to flush the toilet, how to wash and dry hands. You cannot expect to do it for the whole class so taking between six to eight children at a time should make it more manageable. Show how much toilet paper to use and how not to waste the paper. Teach them the importance of checking that the seats are clean and show how to wipe them with paper. Teach and then check that children know how to wash and dry their hands.

Toilets are the often the places where children's behaviour falls short of expectations. Being unsupervised, they may act inappropriately at times. Explain your expectations of their behaviour in the toilets. Explain to them that they will need to tell adults of any problems such as water on the floor or that there is no soap or toilet tissue.

Allow no more than one pupil of each gender at one time to go to the toilet. Some children, especially young ones, may need someone to supervise them initially when they go to the toilet. For that, use your teaching assistant. Also, ask an adult to check if a child, who has been in the toilet for too long, is safe. Ensure though that any adult doing it has had safeguarding and safe working practices training and knows not to enter the toilets alone. If a child has any difficulties in the toilet and needs help, the adults must follow your school procedure. Usually, it is expected that at least two adults who work in school should enter a toilet to help a child if necessary.

Train your children how to let you know when they need to go to the toilet. It should be a straightforward way of putting a hand up. When you work with a group and may not be looking at the class all the time, let your children know that they may come to you and ask for the permission to go to the toilet. This approach will stop children shouting across the classroom asking for permission to go to the toilet.

For monitoring purposes, consider having a pocket chart containing cards with the names of children. The system works like this: when children have been allowed to go to the toilet, they remove the card with their name and place it in the separate 'out' slot. When the children return from the toilet, they remove their card from the 'out' slot and place it back in the pocket chart. The same chart can be used when children go out to interventions or music tuition. This is particularly useful when you have to leave the classroom in the middle of the lesson and another adult comes to cover you. The adult will be able to know which children have left the classroom and are expected to return. To reduce the number of toilet visits during the lessons, use this simple step: before you dismiss the children to break or lunch, remind them to go to the toilet before the lessons start.

At the start of the year, remember to discuss with parents any toileting concerns such as excessive frequency or time. The children presenting with apparent avoidance may be having difficulties they have not shared with you on this potentially sensitive subject. With the very young children, accidents will still occasionally happen. It is prudent to have paper towels or an old cloth to hand to immediately cover accidents if they occur. This means they are not visible for others and you can deal with the child's welfare calmly with minimal attention being drawn. Ensure that the area where the accident took place is properly cleaned - call the caretaker or the school office to sort it out.

A word of advice. You must know and follow your school procedures when dealing with children who have wet or soiled themselves – do not put yourself at risk of having an allegation raised against you. Ask your line manager to explain the school expectations if you are not sure what they are.

LINING UP

Decide on the positions of children in the line and keep rearranging them until you are satisfied. Choose which children are better to be kept apart and how lining up affects the entrance to the classroom. For example, children in front of the line should have their coat pegs the furthest from the door. In this way, those at the end of the line will not be held back waiting to enter while the children at the front are trying to hang their coats. Poor planning of lining up arrangements can at times increase the level of risk by unnecessary and unsafe congestion in the doorway. On the contrary, when you plan carefully, very quickly, children will know the spot in the classroom where they have to stand in the line. So, when you even line up your class group by group or by calling individual names, the children will always stand in their position in the line. The same order you should expect on the playground or in the sports hall when they line up to go to the classroom.

Ensure that your children are calm before attempting to line them up. If they sit on the carpet or are at their desks, especially after an exciting and energetic activity, first calm down your class. To assist you in this, play quiet classical music. Ask the children to close their eyes and imagine what story the music is telling them. Initially, model it yourself by narrating as the music plays.

To line up your class at the end of the PE lesson, use this proven method. Ask children to lie on the floor and close their eyes while you play quiet music. If you do not have music, just describe - calmly and slowly - some wonderful, magical or happy scene. If you do not feel inspired at that point, list the qualities of your class that you admire. On occasions when the children are still restless, guide them on their breathing. Ask them to put their hands on bellies feeling each breath in and out, slowly reducing the volume of your voice. When the children are calm, approach and tap one child at a time on the shoulder. Teach them that it is a signal for that child to line up. To speed up the lining up process, choose up to three children to help you. They will tap on the shoulder the quietest and calmest children on the floor. Expect all children to line up in silence.

You can use the same approach in the classroom. When children are at their desks, play quiet music, ask them to put their arms on the desks and close their eyes. Then, ask the children to rest their heads on their arms on the desks. Select helpers to go around and gently tap on shoulders those who are ready to line up.

When lining up, children may find it difficult to judge the amount of space they need to leave for others in the line. It may cause them being tightly squeezed which in turn can lead to arguments and upsets. To allow sufficient space between the children in the line, teach younger children to space out by putting both hands on the shoulders of the person in front of them. In this ways, they will keep spacing out and readjusting in the line as it grows until everyone is lined up.

Aim to line up quickly and move on without unnecessary delays. Behaviour in the line can deteriorate very rapidly if children stand aimlessly and in close proximity to each other for a long period of time. Forward planning, plenty of practise and consistency will very quickly result in the improvements you seek to establish. Once you have trained your children how to line up, you should expect them to line up in under a minute.

At the start of the year, and occasionally throughout the year, you will need to practise children's lining up skills. For that, select a small group of children to line up. Start with those who you know will be able to model to the rest of the class how to do it very well. Get the class ready and quiet. While looking at them, you can say something like this *I like how quiet and ready Jenny and Michael are. I will ask you both to show the rest of the class how to line up nicely. Please show us how to walk to the line, stand and wait sensibly. You may line up now.* Praise the children and point out what they have done well. Now select the next three or four children to model to the rest of the class. If there is a particular aspect you wish to emphasise on, say what it is you want the children to demonstrate well. You may say, for instance, *Now I want these children to demonstrate how to sensibly use both their hands to make good space for themselves in the line.* After two or three groups have modelled successfully how to line up, proceed with lining up of the remaining children. By this point the rest of the class should be ready to line up although you may continue selecting one group at the time if necessary until everyone has lined up.

To bring in some spirit of competition and team work, tell the class that you would like to see which desk is the tidiest and the readiest to line up. Children will try very hard to be selected. Walk around the classroom and praise at least one thing that stands out at each desk. You can comment on how neat the books are on one of the desks while the other group of children may be sitting quietly and paying attention at another desk. It is important that you allow enough time for this process - especially initially when training your children - before the bell goes off. Holding children back from their break may spoil the positive intention you have planned for this activity.

When the children are calm, quiet and ready, select one

group at the time and ask them to line up. Consider rewarding the group that lines up best. If you have seen an overall improvement in all groups' ability to line up well, tell them how pleased you are – they need to hear it from you. While striving to improve continuously, take the children with you on that journey. They need to feel that their efforts are paying off. So, tell them frequently what improvements you have noticed and make them feel that it is worth trying and working hard.

As you leave the room or the playground with your class, make sure that nobody is left behind. When it is a break or lunch time, take children all the way to the playground. Ensure that there is an adult on the playground duty before you leave your class. If no adult is present, wait for a minute or two. If they are absent for longer than that, send a couple of children to the office to alert the SLT as more classes would be coming out and the playground needs to be supervised.

When you teach younger children, use playful techniques that will engage children to participate. It will help you to manage their movement around the school. One such technique that can be used is the Quiet lions. You can select any other animal for that purpose. The idea is that the children will aim to imitate – silently - the walk of the animal as they move across the school. Be warned though. You have to participate in this too.

When the behaviour in the line is not up to the expected standard, ask the children at the front of the line to stop. The rest of the class will stop as well. Walk along the line and, not to disturb the lessons by loud talking, put your finger on the lips to let them know to be quiet. Whisper compliments to those doing really well or reward them with team points, stickers or table marbles – whatever is appropriate for your class.

Sometimes you need to calm down young children who are already in line and before you leave the classroom. One enjoyable and effective way to do it is to sing *Put your finger on your lips* to the tune of *If you are happy and you know it*. As you begin to approach the end of the song, sing quieter so that you can finish it whispering. The words of the song are given below.

> *Put your finger on your lips, on your lips;*
> *Put your finger on your lips, on your lips;*
> *Put your finger on your lips,*
> *And be quiet on your trips;*
> *Put your finger on your lips,*
> *On your lips.*

SNACK TIME

Provision of snacks must meet at least two key requirements – they must be healthy and be in line with your children's dietary and allergy requirements. When children are admitted in school, make sure that any information concerning their dietary and allergy requirements has been collected and is kept up to date. You must record and act, within reason, on information from parents about their children's dietary needs. Those adults who prepare and serve food must be adequately trained how to do it. Ensure that all adults handling food are aware of your children's allergies. This information should be accessible in the classroom. If you have children who have severe allergies to any of the ingredients or foods you are planning to have in class, change the menu to prevent any risk of exposure of your children to those foods. Special care must be taken when going on trips. Children usually bring their packed lunches for the day. As you do not know what the parents may have put into their children's packed lunch boxes, it is best to closely supervise the children with allergies to prevent them from being exposed to allergens in other children's lunches. If you are in doubt at any point, seek advice from your headteacher or any member of the school leadership team.

Nursery

In nursery, to combine play and snack you can run a snack bar/cafe operated by an adult. With time, try to train the children to independently prepare their own snacks. Children from the age of three should be able to do it.

Open the snack bar at around 10:00-10:30am for 30-45min depending on the size of your nursery. Set out the bar near the kitchen area over the spillage- and slip-proof surface. If your nursery starts at 8:00am then 9:30am should be a better time. For your snack, the choice of milk, water, cheese, apple, carrot sticks and crackers should be sufficient. As children go through the selection, some foods will be more popular and you may need to top them up occasionally. For drinks, place two small plastic jugs – one for milk and the other for water. Have them half-full so that children can pour in the drinks independently. Have a set of plastic bowls and cups for your children to use. Provide a food bin for the leftovers and a large plastic container for the children to place in the used cups and bowls.

The children will need to be trained and supervised for the first two weeks at the beginning of the year. After that time you should expect them to self-serve their snacks. Teach your children how much food and drink to take. You will need to set out the tables where the children are going to have their snacks. Two tables that can facilitate eight children is a manageable number. Monitor the amount of time some children spend at the tables which may force others having to wait for a long time to have a snack.

Train two class helpers who could remind the children to wash hands, pour milk for them and encourage them to eat. It will help to develop their social as well as language skills having to use a range of relevant vocabulary. Pair up a confident child who can speak well with a child who may need to learn those skills.

Teach children to wash their hands before they have their snacks. Allow them to choose a fruit and prepare their own snack under the supervision of an adult. Those children that have finished their snacks can move to the reading corner for a book time. An adult can be positioned there reading books for children.

Give a sticker to each child who has had his or her snack. The benefit is two-fold. You will know who has not had a snack yet and therefore will encourage or remind that child to choose a fruit, vegetable or a drink. Also, the children seeing their friends with stickers will remember to go for a snack. Alternatively, have a pocket chart with children's photos and names. Teach your children to remove their name from one chart and place it into a container once they have collected their snack bowl and a cup. Set them in one line with the names chart being placed between the clean bowls and the trays with food to make sure that the children do not forget to self-register their snack time.

Reception

In reception, the snack time is less complicated than that in the nursery. Children usually have cut up pieces of fruit or vegetable. Sometimes, they can also have milk. At the start of the snack time, settle down your children on the carpet in a circle. Place large trays with snacks somewhere easy to access and not too far from the circle. Teach your children to independently collect the fruit and come to the circle. If you have hand washing facility, train your children to wash their hands first before they collect their snacks. Remember to put a food waste bin near the circle for the children to place the leftovers without having to walk across the classroom to do it. As soon as possible after the snack, a member of staff needs to remove the bin and do the washing up.

The moment when all children are gathered together in a circle is a valuable opportunity to spend time together as a small social group activity led by you. Play calm music, read or tell a story to them. Have a comfortable chair in a circle where any child who has finished eating can sit and tell others a story.

Invite your support staff to participate too. Children need time to talk to others in a structured and calm manner. For you, it is a dedicated time to model how to speak, ask and answer questions in a well-mannered and respectful way. You also have a rich source of assessment opportunities noting the children's achievements and needs necessary for your future planning. Often, it is the learning when children think that they are just playing that has the most profound impact on them. This social time will also prove to be enjoyable for you, the teacher.

END OF THE DAY

Chaos in the midst of chaos isn't funny, but chaos in the midst of order is.

STEVE MARTIN

The end of the school day is as important as its beginning. It may be argued that both are the most important parts of the day. Well prepared and efficiently run beginning of the day can help you set the children in the right mood for learning for the rest of the day. Equally, well-executed end of the day can help them leave the school with positive impressions about their experiences during that day.

SUMMING UP THE DAY

Summing up the day has three benefits. First, the prospect of doing the summary at the end of the day encourages you to plan and run the day well. Secondly, the process of summing up leads you to a better evaluation of the day. Thirdly, the succinct summary helps your pupils to understand

and remember what they have learned, what they did well and what they need to do better.

You need an orderly procedure when summing up the day. For that, settle down the young children on the carpet - the older ones would be more comfortable at their desks. The following points are examples of what you can typically cover. With adjustments, however, they would apply equally well to any lesson or activity you wish to summarise.

SUMMING UP WHAT HAS BEEN LEARNED

Above all, be concise. The more long-winded your summary, the greater the risk of confusing the children. In a few brief points, sum up the most important skills that have been learned that day. Consider the following two versions of a text – the summary of the day. The teacher lists the activities from literacy. What makes the edited version more suitable and purposeful? Above all, the focus on the learned skills, not the generic statements and listing of activities. Statements in the first version add nothing to reinforce or extend learning.

First version

> *Today in literacy we learned how to make sandwiches. I hope you have enjoyed the lesson. You designed your sandwiches and made them independently. You worked very hard as a team and your behaviour was excellent. Your parents should be very proud of you.*

Second version

> *In literacy you learned to choose three healthy ingredients for your sandwiches. You know how to hold a knife safely when cutting tomatoes and spreading butter. You now remember to wash your hands before cooking. Tell your parents about it tonight and ask if you can make them a healthy sandwich at home.*

If you want to point out particularly good examples of behaviour or work, tell your children what exactly makes them stand out: I particularly liked the work of the Green table in Science. They tested the impact of different fluids on friction between two solids. They used the collected data to back up their conclusion. Children also explained the difference between their conclusion and the hypothesis.

As you share your evaluation of the day, give your children a minute to reflect on one or two new things they have learned during the day. Model for them how to reflect and to distinguish between what they did and what they learned. It is what they have learned that matters here most.

SAY WHAT NEEDS TO IMPROVE

Do not introduce new things or try to explain or clarify something at the end of the day. Say in strong, memorable phrases or sentences one or two things you want children to improve. Don't be content with open-ended statements such as I want you to focus on your work better.

How much better? Instead, formulate your point precisely. It has to be simple but important - something that the children can do immediately the following day. Here is one example. From tomorrow, everyone will need to produce at least one page of writing within the first 20min of independent work.

Refrain here from evaluating shortcomings of individuals or groups. The points you list have to apply to all children, or at least to the majority of the class. Avoid focusing on the behaviour all the time and risk turning this activity into criticism. Be constructive; you can always discuss the behaviour during circle times.

SENDING THEM HAPPY

Your conclusion to the day needs to be memorable. After all, this is what the children hear and see last. This will be in their minds when they go home; it will be a pleasant experience for the parents having a conversation with children about their school day.

To get the best out of children, you need to motivate them – fill them with enthusiasm and desire to impress you. Different children are motivated by different things. For some, to earn a sticker is exciting. For others, a short note home expressing your appreciating of the determination or celebrating the progress is something worthwhile their effort. Others, though not indifferent to rewards, have high expectations of themselves and may not value everyday praise. For them, what matters most is that their learning experiences are challenging and interesting and that you know them well as individuals. A quiet word of your acknowledgement during the lesson from time to time may be sufficient to keep them motivated to learn and succeed.

There is hardly a day in school without some challenges in the classroom or the playground. Even if there were problems during the day, discuss what can be learned from them. Reassure the children and make them look forward to having a fresh start the following day.

Send them off with something motivational and awe-inspiring; make them feel good about themselves and have something to aspire to. There are plenty of online resources – quotes, images or video resources – which would make this part easy to plan for.

If fitting, tell them one or two good things you have planned for the following day; give them something to look forward to.

GETTING READY TO LEAVE

It is better to be early than late although the extremes in each case are not desirable. When you approach the end of the day, the activities should naturally be aligned to flow into a successful conclusion of the day. When the bell goes off, you and your children should be ready to leave the classroom. The bell itself is only a signal that the school day is over, not that it is time to pack up. Keep in mind the parents waiting outside to collect their children. Many of them have different engagements and can get irritated by waiting for their child being brought out late. What can make matters worse is that the children forgetting something. It then forces parents to want to talk to you about it. And, as you are dismissing the class at that time, it begins to affect you and delays the dismissal. It is easy for such situations to spin out of control and create undesirable confrontation between the parents and you. If you are constantly harassed, running from one place to another trying to finish everything you have planned, never have enough time for all you need to do, the chances are you are not managing your time well. Unless you address it, it is likely to lead to you getting stressed or slip up. It then may force the school leaders to step in to see what is going on. You can and should avoid it.

One of the basic rules that will help you be in control is to organise in advance and manage your day. When you plan your day, plan each session from the end. In this way you will be certain to finish it on time as you have intended.

One can often observe class teachers planning excessively and do too much during the main teaching activity. The result of such approach is not surprising – the teachers spend too much time teaching and the children do not have enough time to learn. Planning from the end, gives you an opportunity not to make this error. For each part of your day, estimate the time that you think is necessary. Then, plan what you or the children should achieve by the end of each part. Here is a simple example of what your plan for the last part of the day may look like:

Time	Activity	Duration
3:05pm	Collecting belongings	3min
3:08pm	Homework, letters	4min
3:12pm	Summing up the day	3min
3:15pm	Putting coats on	3min
3:18pm	Lining up, leaving the classroom	2min
3:20pm	Dismissal	

HOMEWORK

The day in school is very structured and children have plenty to do to keep them busy and stimulated. When the school day is over though, many of them would like to do something at home. Not only is it beneficial for children to learn independently and pursue own interests, it helps you, the teacher, to cover many areas which may be not possible to do in school.

Tell the children what they could do at home - it may be the times tables your class have to learn, or the spellings for that week; or, it can be the need to practise handwriting or read a book. Share with the children and parents your school website where you have useful links with educational content for children to use at home.

Promote independent learning for older children. Encourage project work or investigation to carry out at home. encourage children to bring their projects to school to share with others. Don't be content with a scrappy sheet of paper and some facts copied or printed out from the internet. Set your expectations of the research and presentation standards high. Display children's projects in class and ask them to share their work with the rest of their class. Initially, you may have only a few children. As you talk about the work at home regularly, praise and celebrate the outcomes, thank parents for helping the children – the effect will soon be transformational. Very quickly not only the children but their parents too will want to compete and get engaged in home learning knowing that it is beneficial for their children and that it brings a great sense of joy and satisfaction.

Whatever the activity, children need to want to do it and not see it as a chore. Only then you can be sure that they learn at home without you having to monitor it. Ask your children if they have library cards. If you have a public library nearby, and your children do not access it, arrange regular class trips. The librarians will show the children how to access the library and share interesting books or digital resources on offer. The trip can also be an opportunity to collect permission slips to ensure that all children get their own library cards during the visit. For some, particularly in areas of high deprivation, this can be the pupils' only access to the internet or a sole source of books for their areas of interest.

Ensure your class are confident using the library. Do not presume that every parent is familiar with it either. The libraries may have changed significantly since parents used them as children, or simply be a place where they have never been confident.

LETTERS

Letters are essential in communication between the school and its families: you may be required to send a letter detailing the class trip arrangements, telling the parents about the upcoming events, or simply passing on a weekly school newsletter. Do not presume though that having given out the letters to children there is a guarantee that all parents will read or see them.

If the children are taking trip letters home and need to bring permission slips back, tell them about it. If it is a field trip and they need to wear suitable clothes and footwear which you have listed in your letter, ask the children to remind their parents about it. In other instances, go through the letters detailing such things as the costume arrangements for the class assembly, payment for a trip or tuition, the opening times of the school fair and so on.

If you have any families who may find it difficult to read letters in English, read them to the children and ask to explain to the parents what to do. Alternatively, ask one of the parents who may speak the same language to assist that parent.

ACCIDENT SLIPS

Sometimes children have accidents at school and a first aid note usually is sent home. Place the note in the child's bag and make sure the parents know about it. When the incident is serious, such as a bumped head, ensure that you tell the parents about it and ask them to keep an eye on the child (enquire if a phone call has already been made by a First Aider if they directly return a child to you). Not all children are collected by their parents at the end of the day. If the child goes to an after school club or is collected by a childminder, ask that adult to monitor the child and pass on the message to the parents about the accident and the slip in the bag. You may decide to call the parents yourself if it would be better to explain the circumstances surrounding the incident. When you do, explain what happened and reassure the parent that you have dealt with it. If appropriate, tell them what measures will be put in place to reduce the likelihood of such incidents happening in the future. Such short curtesy call can go a long way in establishing a good rapport with parents and preventing unnecessary stress or possible formal complaints the following day.

Then back yourself up by making a record in which you note down the details of your conversation with the parents. It is an especially important habit when you are a school middle or senior leader and discuss these matters with parents in your leadership capacity. In this case, follow up your conversation with a carefully worded letter summarising the main points of the conversation with the parent, any parental concerns that were raised and what you will do to address them. Needless to say, you must be careful not to write anything factually inaccurate – stick to the established facts and follow the school procedures.

COLLECTING BELONGINGS

Most adults forget to do something from time to time. Children also do it, only more frequently. At the end of the school day, children often need to take many things home and you need to remind them about it. So, make sure that they take their reading books home and that they have collected their homework, water bottles and packed lunch boxes. Encourage your children to look after each other and prompt their peers to remember to collect their belongings.

Frequently, children misplace their jumpers, coats, hats or any other belongings they have in school. It is sometimes surprising what they can manage to lose. Schools usually have a lost property area where such items are placed when found. If necessary, send the children who are looking for the misplaced jumper or a coat to the lost property with a teaching assistant. Children can go there alone if they are old enough or, you can remind children to go the lost property area with their parent at the end of the day. Don't leave it until the end of the day to deal with the lost items. Whenever your children alert you of something they have misplaced, find quiet times during the day which would be least disruptive and seek to locate the lost items then.

It often happens that other children by mistake pick up someone else's piece of clothing and take it home. You will save a lot of time and unnecessary distress caused by the lost pieces if you ask the parents to label their children's clothes – name and class - with a laundry pen, preferably in an obvious place such as inside the collar.

PUTTING ON COATS

While in summer coats are not an issue, during the colder months they can be a cause of delays. To manage the process of coat collection at the end of the day efficiently, ask your children to stay at their desks and send one table at the time to get their coats. The children should put them on and come back to the desks. The rest of the class can read a book quietly until they have been called. For the very young children, put on a video or an audio story, or play a nursery rhyme on the screen. Children of infant age may need help with their coats, scarves and hats. Ask your teaching assistant to oversee this and assist them if necessary. Check that the coats are buttoned up or zipped up and that the children wear their hats in winter before you go outside. Children who can do their zips often love helping their classmates. Encourage and praise this when they do it kindly and calmly.

Collecting belongings and putting on coats are the activities that do not need to be sequential. Ask your children also to collect their packed lunches, book bags and homework when they go to take their coats.

ORDERLY DISMISSAL

Generally, children are dismissed from either seated position – carpet or desks, or standing one – from a line or a group. Some schools may give teachers a choice in this while others may insist on a particular way of doing it. Whatever your arrangements - chosen or directed - some general helpful principles apply to both.

The end of the day is usually a very busy time and your dismissal arrangements need to be well planned to be safe, efficient and smooth. Safety of your children is paramount so when dismissing children to their parents position yourself in such a way that you always stand between the parents and the children - there needs to be a large enough gap for you to see every child that goes from you to the parents. With very young children, hand over each child personally to the parent. Ensure that children are calm and that they can hear and see you calling them. If you have an additional adult, consider directing that adult to manage the process of calling the names while you can have an opportunity to have a quick word with the parent.

DISMISSING TO THE RIGHT PERSON

Your school should have the names of people who are permitted to collect the children. Apart from the parents, you can only dismiss children to these adults. If a parent tells you in the morning that someone else would be picking up the child that afternoon, ask the parent to tell you what the person looks like and to confirm his or her name. Some schools ask parents to give a password in the event that another person has been authorised by the parent to collect the child. These passwords are usually in the main office.

If in doubt, do not dismiss the child. Take the adult with

the child to the office and call the parent to confirm that it is the person authorised to collect their child. If necessary, ask the parent to talk to that adult on the phone to make sure it is the correct person.

Have a list of your children and the names of persons authorised to collect them – if possible tick off who collects them on the day. It is especially helpful in large city schools with high mobility pupils when you may not know all parents or family members collecting the children. In nursery, consider asking for photographs of regular adults collecting the children. Display the photographs near the door against the names of the children in the nursery. This approach will help when the school has high mobility staffing or cover arrangements involving different adults who may not know the families.

Occasionally, you cannot dismiss some children for different reasons. One such reason is that the social services asked the school not to let the child go home the child and wait for their officer to arrive at school. You should be guided by your school leaders what to do in these circumstances. If in doubt, check with your headteacher or another senior member of the school leadership team for guidance.

Sometimes a court order may prevent one of the parents from being with the child. In these cases make sure the school office has confirmed with you that they have seen a copy of the order. Be certain that you know what the parent looks like if you have not met that parent. Ask your school leaders for guidance in these specific cases before you make a decision to dismiss a pupils to the parent who may not be permitted to collect their child.

CHILDREN NOT COLLECTED ON TIME

Follow your school procedures for children who are picked up late. It can be, for example, taking them to the school office or the after school club. Do not create expectations that you will wait for the parents. Avoid staying alone in the class or playground with a child when you need to be elsewhere, even when you understand the parents' genuine reasons. You can of course stay with a child in the office or after school club if you feel the child needs your reassurance.

AFTER SCHOOL CLUBS

Not every child goes home at the end of the school day. If your school provides a wide range of after school activities, it is likely that some of your children will be attending them. It means that their parents will only come to collect them at the end of those activities.

Have a list of children who go to different clubs on any day. It will help you to distinguish between the children that have not been collected and those who are going to the after school activities. Some children may forget that they are supposed to go to an after school club or, if they go to a few during the week, which club to go to. The list would be a helpful guide for you to remind these children where to go.

If a group of your children is collected from your class

by another adult, ask that group to let you know when the adult has arrived to collect them so that you see which children are leaving the classroom. If you are expected to take the children to the room where the after school club is run, keep those children waiting for you to dismiss the rest of the class and then take them to the club. Alternatively, ask your teaching assistant to escort the children to the after school club. Older children usually can go independently to the clubs through the school.

A FINAL WORD

Thank you for taking time to choose, read and finish this book.

Regardless of their level or experience, the mark of good teachers is the ability to reflect and evolve intellectually and in their own practice. Teaching is a profession of change. It will always continue to test your skills of adaptability. In seeking and reading this book, we trust that have put yourself to that expectation.

Printed in Great Britain
by Amazon